Pressing My Luck

Pressing My Luck
A Doctor's Lottery Journey

To Miss Emily
It was wonderful seeing
you again. Best of luck,
Shirley

Shirley Press, MD

This book is non-fiction. A few names have been changed.

Published in the United States by Re-Spin Publishing

ISBN: 978-0-9894061-0-9

ISBN-978-0-9894061-0-9

Special acknowledgement is made to the following:

Original cover art by Mercedes Diaz

Due to the variable conditions, materials, and individual skills, the publisher, author, editor, translator, transcriber, and/or designer disclaim any liability for loss or injury resulting from the use or interpretation of any information presented in this publication.

While every effort has been made in the preparation of this material to ensure the information is accurate, the publisher, author, editor, translator, and/or transcriber assume no responsibility for errors and/or omissions. No liability is assumed for damages resulting from the use of the information contained herein.

For Sarah who brings sunshine to my life.

CONTENTS

Foreword: First Impressions

When I was helping my mother move to an independent living facility we had to part with many of her things. She was going from a 2,200 square foot house to a 700 square foot apartment. At the time, I thought about what is left behind at the end of one's life besides memories and photographs. My mother is a Holocaust survivor. Her life story is preserved in video interviews conducted by two organizations that document the lives of those who survived the horrors of Nazi Germany. These videotapes are her legacy. Her life is inspiring. While my life pales in comparison, I also would like to share and inspire. Plain and simple, that's why I've written this book.

After diagnosing otitis media (ear infection) over 15,000 times, I came to the conclusion that I am more than ready to try something new. Summoning the perseverance that saw me through medical school and residency in pediatrics, I applied myself to writing this book (although, it has actually taken me longer to finish than the four years of medical school). This work contains a lifetime of thoughts, experiences and perhaps some of my ego demanding its due after years of being suppressed by my shyness.

In a nutshell, this is my life. There are happy days, funny events, depressing and desperate times, revelations and a lot of coincidences. It's a convoluted American dream in a lot of ways. Between the lines, I seek to find my special place and purpose in this world. One of my biggest fears in life is to be unmemorable or invisible.

Like many aspiring authors, I've been writing this book for much longer than I ever expected. To bend a well-known phrase; dying is easy; it's writing that's tough. Sometimes, I have ideas that evaporate before I write them down. I'm still working as a physician. I get distracted by life which consumes the time I vowed to dedicate to my book.

However, I finally got the jolt I needed when I was required to take a vision test and renew my driver's license a few years ago. As the clerk handed me my new license, I asked, "When do I have to renew again?" She replied, "Eight years." I was aghast. In eight years, I was going to be 66. I knew it was time to reinvent myself. I made a resolution not to waste any more time. Of course, this is impossible, but I am trying.

I considered writing a memoir before I won the lottery. There was my chance encounter with the essence of Paul McCartney, a total fantasy for a die-hard Beatles fan, though I couldn't see that it would amount to much more than a three to four page story. Then I considered writing about the Pediatric ER and learning more about my parents' early lives. However, with working long hours and raising a family, I never found the time. I thought I'd get to it when I went part-time or retired.

Then it happened. In 2001, I was your typical, hardworking, pediatric emergency room doctor ... until I won 56 million dollars (17.5 million take home) in the Florida Lottery with a ticket that I bought in the hospital's gift shop. It gave me the time needed to write and it cast a new light on everything. There have been unintended consequences to winning the lottery and the money has not prevented my family from facing despairing times. Yet the lottery has led to new experiences, such as wading into the South Florida charity scene, figuring out how to fend off scammers, meeting new people and harboring the admittedly juvenile feelings of payback that come into play. The win has also enabled me to expand my life and perspective in surprising ways.

As a little girl, I always dreamed about being rich, or rather, dreamed about not being poor. I thought if I was driven – studied hard, earned college scholarships, and picked the right career – I would be successful. And that's what happened. By the time I was 50, I had pretty much accomplished my goals, but also felt resigned that most of my major adventures were behind me. Then, my secret fantasy came true – I won the lottery. My polyester life turned to silk.

So I hope people will enjoy sharing my adventures and perhaps learn something along the way. I want the lessons learned in my life to be part of my legacy. With my writing, I hope to make a lasting impression.

1. Ticket To Ride

As a doctor I'm well aware that the unexpected doesn't come pre-announced. A person doesn't wake up in the morning thinking, I'm going to wind up in the emergency room today or I'm going to have a car sideswipe me as I cross the street at lunchtime. As it turns out, the same thing is true when good fortune pulls up a seat at your dinner table.

I was aware that there would be a drawing on the night of September 5, 2001 for what was at that point the largest lottery jackpot in Florida's history. I fully intended to buy a few tickets that day, as I did nearly every week, but I wasn't sure I'd be able to fit it in. I worked a short shift in the ER that morning treating patients, took a mandatory course on blood borne pathogens right after that, and then had to race back to my office to deal with the mountain of paperwork that had been collecting all day.

At the time, I was the director of a pediatric emergency department and surprisingly many people were under the impression that I did nothing but attend meetings from nine to five. Besides seeing patients, the endlessly growing pile of documents to review, messages to read and calls to return attested to something very different. After I completed the course, I needed immediate documentation of my attendance so I had to take extra time after the class was over to get that from the lecturer. I really didn't have a spot in my schedule to buy lottery tickets, but since I played the lottery so often, it seemed ludicrous for me not to participate in such an enormous jackpot.

The sprawling Jackson Memorial Hospital complex included an arcade with a variety of shops, including a gift shop that sold the tickets. I ducked in on my way back from the lecture and sighed heavily when I saw a line of around 10 people ahead of me, all waiting for the single cashier to help them out. This gift shop was never crowded, even when the hospital was very busy. It became immediately apparent that the huge lottery drawing was the reason everyone was lined up here that day.

"I'm gonna get myself a gigantic house when I win," said one woman to another while they waited.

"I'm gonna have steak every night," the other replied dreamily.

The man in front of them turned in their direction. "I have my eyes on a Maserati. A black one with lots of chrome."

They all grinned and continued to expand on their fantasies. I could tell from their ID badges that they were workers at the hospital. A part of me wanted to join in on their musing, but I didn't. I was wearing a lab coat and was obviously a doctor, and they probably figured I didn't belong in the line in the first place. Most people, even those who work closely with us, are under the impression that all doctors are wealthy. Even though that's far from true, I felt a little bit out of place.

"I'm gonna get my kids back," said the woman directly in front of me. Everyone turned in her direction. She told the group that she'd lost her six children due to neglect, but that once she hit it big on the lottery, the family would be together again. That sounded better to me than throwing a few hundred thousand after a car, though the mention of neglect made me wonder if any amount of money could make that family whole.

I didn't consider what I would do with all the cash. Since I'd never won anything in my life, and the odds of winning that night's drawing were one in twenty million, I assumed my losing streak would continue. I just liked to play. What I did think about was everything I had to do when I got back to my office, along with wondering about crises that might have emerged in my absence. The woman behind the counter was doing the best she could, but she seemed to be moving very slowly. Twice while I was waiting, I considered getting out of the line, but I stood my ground. Once I got close enough to see that the store had York Peppermint Patties in stock that day – they're my favorite candy – my resolve strengthened.

When it was finally my turn, I put a Peppermint Patty on the counter and asked for six Quick Pick tickets. I'd read somewhere that more people won the lottery by having the computer randomly spit out numbers than by choosing their own, so I always played this way. I stuck the tickets with my six sets of numbers in my lab coat pocket, opened the candy wrapper and headed back up to work.

As anticipated, there was a tremendous amount of work for me to attend to when I got back to my office. I literally had to squeeze in a full day's worth of administrative duties in the few hours I had left that afternoon. The tickets as well as that evening's Lotto drawing were soon forgotten.

When I got home, a different swirl of activity awaited me. A quick family dinner. Coaxing my teenaged kids through their homework.

Relaxing in front of the television for a while. Taking care of a few household chores. At some point, the drawing for the largest lottery jackpot in Florida history happened but it was the furthest thing from my mind.

"Dr. Press, did you hear that someone from Jackson won the lottery?" a nurse said to me as I walked into the clean utility room the next morning.

"Wow," I said, my eyes widening. "Who is it?"

"No one knows. The winner hasn't come forward yet. All we know is that the winning ticket came from the gift shop."

I wondered if it could have been one of my line mates. Maybe it was the woman with the six kids. I continued to assume it wasn't me, because I didn't have that kind of luck. In fact, though I'd been playing the Florida lottery for as long as I could remember, I'd never had a winning of more than nine dollars.

Several others joined us at that point, and the speculation began on who it might be and what it was going to do to their lives. As the conversation continued, I tried to imagine how sudden wealth would affect someone.

"That person is going to be such an oddball," I said during a lull. "They're not going to be able to fit in anywhere."

As the day went on, a rumor gained momentum that Carl in the key shop was the winner. He hadn't come to work and this was clearly an indicator that he'd cashed in and was off scouting a beachfront mansion. When he came in a few hours later, the speculation moved on. It was fascinating to see how this story captivated my colleagues. At some point, some new information broke: the winner had bought six tickets at the gift shop yesterday.

That was the first time I started to consider the possibility that I could be the winner. Surely, I wasn't the only person who'd bought exactly six tickets at the gift shop yesterday. Still, it narrowed down the crowd. Of course, I could have ended the mystery by checking my tickets, but I thought I'd left them at home on my desk not realizing that I had been spending the entire day with the equivalent of fifty-six million dollars in my lab coat pocket.

The hospital was swirling with activity and I wound up working late. By the time I got home, my husband and children had eaten already. I went upstairs to check my desk where I always left the tickets. The tickets weren't where I thought I'd left them, which gave me a little surge of panic. I could not find them. I raced around the house like a cat on catnip frantically looking for the tickets. As much as I'd convinced myself that I couldn't possibly be the winner, the chance was still there. What if I'd managed to misplace the winning ticket? I looked through my pocketbook. There were Tic Tacs, Double Mint Gum and salt packets but no tickets. I gave up and sat down for dinner, reading that morning's *Miami Herald* and eating my microwaved Stouffer's frozen entrée. I mused again on the possibility of being the winner since no one had come forward to claim the gigantic jackpot and then quickly reminded myself that this kind of luck didn't run in my family. The biggest prize any of us had ever landed was the case of baked beans my father had won many years ago at a grocer's picnic.

During the meal, I had a fleeting thought that the tickets could quite possibly be in my lab coat. Once I finished dinner I found my lab coat hanging on the hall tree. Of course! I reached into a pocket and pulled out the ticket. Search over. They had been in the top pocket the entire time and I had not even bothered to look at them.

I got the morning paper and went through my usual ticket checking routine. I covered the last three numbers of the six rows of numbers and checked the first three against the newspaper. I did this every week, because the only way a person could be a big winner was to have these first three numbers match. Otherwise, the payouts were tiny (in other words, the kinds of payouts that I knew). Of course, my numbers never matched. However, this week was an exception. The first three numbers of the winner were 3, 9, and 10. One of my rows of numbers on the ticket started with 3, 9, and 10.

My heart jumped just a little. A fleeting thought hit. "Wow, could it be?" I knew the tickets were sold in the gift shop. I knew that there was one winner. I knew-- stop it -- I laughed out loud at the thought. *Never, not me!*

I froze; my heart was pounding not wanting to reveal the second three numbers. I chuckled again and uncovered them - 24, 33, and 35. I must have looked like a Looney Tunes cartoon character with my eyes bugging out. They were wandering left to right to left to right, focusing on the newspaper and then back to the ticket. They matched. Then I checked it again and again. My eyes weren't playing tricks on me: the numbers in the paper matched the numbers on my ticket. I was the winner of the $56.37 million dollar jackpot!

My legs felt wobbly as I made my way down to the family room, trying to remain as calm as possible.

"Um, Bill, I think I won the lottery," I said to my husband.

He looked away from the television and tipped his head toward me. "You're tired, Shirley. You didn't win the lottery."

I had the ticket and the newspaper in my hand and I held it out to him. "I'm pretty sure I did."

My daughter Sarah was sitting on the couch with him. With a groan, she got up and came over to me, taking the items from my hands. She examined both carefully and then did a double take.

Then she screamed at such a volume that I'm surprised the neighbors didn't call the police.

"She won! She won! Mom won!"

When she started screaming, I started screaming, as though I hadn't entirely believed it myself until I had a second opinion. My son Gershon got up to join us, needing to confirm this for himself. When he did, he started screaming as well. Someone listening upstairs might have thought that our family room floor had suddenly turned into a pit of snakes. That would have been a more likely scenario than the one that was actually playing out.

Bill had no choice now but to acknowledge that this was not a product of my tired eyes. He examined the paper and the ticket himself and his face went white. For the next several minutes, all he could say was, "Are you kidding me? Are you kidding me?"

This lightheaded moment lasted for at least fifteen minutes. Finally, though, it dawned on us that we had no idea what to do next. Obviously, we couldn't take the ticket over to the gift shop for redemption. Something told me that they didn't have fifty-six million dollars in their cash register. Having no better plan, we called Michael Dribin, a former neighbor and the only attorney we knew. Though we used to live only a couple of houses away from each other, we'd never really become friends. We'd say hello at the synagogue on occasion, but that was about it. As a result, it took a minute for Michael to remember us. Of course, what we told him after that guaranteed that he'd never forget us again.

Michael naturally had no experience with the procedures involved in collecting a huge lottery jackpot. However, he said he could make some calls for us and that he would get back to us as soon as he could.

We got off the phone and waited. I was rippling with energy, not sure what to do with myself. I'd had several life defining experiences like my father's death when I was 18, graduating medical school, having children, but nothing I'd gone through in the past prepared me for something like this.

"We're going to be millionaires," I said, shaking my head in wonder.

Gershon seemed especially pleased about this. "Now I can finally get my own car," said my seventeen year old. Sarah talked excitedly while Bill just seemed dumbstruck. I knew exactly how he felt.

Michael called back an hour later, though it felt as though days had passed. He told us that we had to photocopy the front and back of the ticket, put the original in a safe deposit box, and give him the copy so he could start the verification process with the state. It was too late to do any of this that night, so we had no choice but to set the entire winning-the-lottery thing aside for the rest of the night. It goes without saying that I had more than a little trouble getting to sleep. I took the ticket to bed with me.

The next morning, Bill and I arrived at the Miami Beach Public Library a half-hour before it opened. As we waited, I grew increasingly anxious. I imagined that everyone could tell that we had a massively valuable piece of paper in our possession and that there were muggers lurking behind every corner. When the doors finally opened, we dashed to the photocopy machine only to learn that we couldn't get the thing to work. In increasingly louder whispers, Bill and I tried to coach each other through the process, but we failed. Finally, feeling horribly conspicuous, we asked for assistance. When two members of the library staff also struggled, I felt a little better. Still, I couldn't help imagining one of these people – who were probably scrupulously honest – making a mad dash with our ticket.

A third staff member finally got the machine to work for us and we had our photocopies. If any of the people who assisted us had any idea of what we were copying, they gave no indication of it. So much for the neon sign reading "new lottery millionaire" I imagined flashing on and off above my head.

We secured the ticket in our safe deposit box and then brought a copy to Michael. He looked at the document as though it were a rare coin or an alien life form. This was definitely not what he thought he'd be dealing with this week when he woke up yesterday morning. It was Friday morning September 7 and the weekend was rapidly approaching.

"I'll get to work on this right away," he said. "Meanwhile, don't tell anyone about it until I find out more from the state."

How does one keep this kind of secret completely to one's self? I couldn't possibly do it. As soon as I got to a phone, I delivered the news to my mother and sister. My sister responded with the ecstatic screaming I'd become so familiar within the last twelve hours.

My mother didn't scream, though. She listened to what I was telling her very calmly and then said, "Oh, I knew we would win one day. I always thought it was going to be me." It became clear to me immediately that she wasn't talking about winning something in a vague sense; she'd genuinely imagined that one day she would win the lottery. That it had, as she put it, "skipped a generation" just meant that her vision had been off by the slightest bit. This fascinated me, and I've subsequently noticed it from many other people with modest financial means. It's a sense that things are going to get exponentially better soon.

I suppose that's encouraging in a way, even though it's nothing but an illusion for most. It certainly worked out for my mother.

Work that day was a complete blur. People were of course still speculating about Jackson's big winner, and I did my best to participate in a few of these conversations to keep suspicion away from me. Fortunately, I had that ever present pile of paperwork to deal with in addition to my usual administrative duties. These gave me something else to concentrate on, and I did my best to throw myself into my work.

The next day was a Saturday and I had lunch scheduled with my friend Cheryl Levin. I'd known Cheryl for a long time, and I was sure she could read something into my fidgeting and distraction. I tried to keep up my end of the conversation, but I'm guessing that I did a lousy job of it and that Cheryl could tell that something was on my mind.

I'd picked Cheryl up for lunch. On the car ride back to her place, she said, "Did you hear that someone from Jackson won the Lotto?"

"Yeah, I know," I said. "Everyone's talking about it."

She leaned toward me. "Was it you?"

"No," I said, waving the thought away casually. Inside, though, I felt awful about lying to a good friend. I switched subjects quickly and hoped that Cheryl would think nothing of it.

Bill and I had a dinner date that evening with our friends Kay and Leo Edelsberg, who we'd known forever. As we ate, I wondered if my winning the lottery was going to change our relationship. That would have been devastating to me, and I vowed to do everything in my power to prevent money from driving a wedge between us and our close friends and family.

Not telling them the news was driving me crazy, and I could tell that Bill was equally tormented. We kept sharing wary glances across the table. I thought we were keeping this between us, but when we insisted on picking up the check, we crossed a line.

"Okay, something is going on," Kay said, looking in my direction.

I glanced up at Bill, and he rolled his eyes, which I took as his permission.

I chuckled and then turned to Kay. "We won the lottery."

Kay's eyes exploded out of their sockets. "The big one?"

I shook my head and let out a little squeal. Our friends were all over us at that point. I was so glad they were reacting this way. I was worried they might be jealous or might suddenly feel awkward around us. Of course, they had no problem with our picking up the check after that.

I felt guilty about Cheryl. I called her that night and left a message for her to call back. When she phoned the next day, I was out food shopping.

Bill answered the phone and said, "Shirley feels really guilty that she lied to you."

"About what?" a bewildered Cheryl replied.

"She won," Bill said.

"Oh my God, oh my God," yelled Cheryl.

On Sunday September 9, we had a barbecue to attend at the home of another ER doctor. Why couldn't this have been one of those weekends where we had nothing to do? For the third time in two days, I had to navigate through a social event without spouting off about our new fortune. In some ways it should have been easier to keep my mouth shut in this setting, since we were with colleagues rather than close friends. However, it turned out to be much harder. The conversation at the barbecue continued to revolve around who bought the winning ticket at our gift shop. One of the doctors in attendance inadvertently took some of the pressure off of me when he suggested to several people at the party that he had a big announcement to make the next day. Word spread immediately around the gathering that this doctor might be the big winner, and I certainly didn't do anything to allay those rumors. And there I was wondering what could his secret be? The next morning, he told everyone that he was stepping down from his role as the Director of the Medical Emergency Room to focus on being an ER attending physician.

I somehow managed to get through that Monday without the big neon sign above my head creating a frenzy at the hospital. Then, shortly after I got home from work, Michael called.

"You've been confirmed," he said, meaning that the state acknowledged that we seemed to have a legitimate claim to the winnings based on the appearance of the photocopy and the written statement we'd included about how I'd bought the ticket. The next step was for us to bring the ticket to the lottery offices in Tallahassee for official confirmation. Michael told Bill that he was booking flights for us for Wednesday morning, and that he would accompany us. When Bill hung up, the four of us started screaming again. Now, we just had to make it until Wednesday.

That was the evening of September 10, 2001. By the next morning, no one was speculating on the Florida lottery winner anymore.

So much has been written already about people's reactions to 9/11, and certainly there was nothing unusual about my own reaction to the horror. I was about a block away from my house when I heard the news, and I turned around so I could watch some of the coverage at home. It soon dawned on me that the hospital would be on alert during a crisis of this magnitude and I got back in my car to get to my office quickly. As I drove, I felt tremendously guilty. I'd been blessed by an incredible stroke of luck, but many good people had just been killed by fortune's dark twin.

The lottery wasn't on anyone's mind that day. We all tried to push through with our work, but doing so felt harder than it had ever felt before. I remember almost nothing about the day at the hospital except for one notable exchange. One of our patients, Michelle, was receiving a round of treatment for leukemia at the clinic. She'd been undergoing treatment for a while, and her mother Tracye and I had become friendly. Tracye was understandably anxious about her little girl's condition. That day, I went to visit them at the clinic.

While doctors treated Michelle, Tracye and I sat in pint-sized chairs and talked about what had happened in New York, DC, and Pennsylvania. Tracye, who was already carrying the nearly unbearable burden of her daughter's illness, seemed positively weighed down by this new tragedy.

"Man, I could really use some good news today," she said.

Something told me that sharing with Tracye was the right thing to do. We both needed a tiny glimmer of light during that dark day. As guilty as I felt and as concerned as I was about Tracye's taking it the wrong way, I told her about my winning the lottery.

Tracye screamed and jumped for joy. She hugged and kissed me, and we both began to cry. Tracye told me that this was the best thing she'd heard in a long time and that she thought I was deserving of it. I had no idea how anyone deserved to win the lottery, but I was thrilled with her reaction. It made this mournful day a little less awful. (Michelle and Tracye's story has a happy ending. The treatment worked, and Michelle remains cancer-free. She went on to college and has recently started working as a nurse. Tracye and I are still friends ten years later.)

Michael called that night to talk about our trip to Tallahassee. He said there was never going to be a good time to travel over the next few weeks and that we may as well get it over with. All air traffic was grounded for almost a week. We decided to drive instead. Michael was unable to accompany us so he referred us to an attorney friend of his in that area.

Two days later, Bill and I headed off on the most unexpected road trip of our lives. Being a little suspicious that someone might be following us, Bill decided to rent a car instead of using our own. With map in hand (no GPS back then), we made our way on the arduous ten hour drive to Tallahassee with paranoia as our constant companion. What if someone was following us? I kept my eye on the road the whole time, looking for stalkers. We purposely stayed overnight at a Holiday Inn. After all, what kind of millionaire would choose a Holiday Inn? I kept the original ticket clutched tightly in my hand and made sure that the hotel door would never be opened. No room service that night!

The following morning we arrived in Tallahassee and met with Michael's attorney friend at the lottery office to claim the reward. It was a surreal experience. Though it was business as usual for the lottery workers, I felt like I was a criminal being interrogated in the *Twilight Zone*.

It was a step-by-step process. First, I was escorted into a cold, non-descript room where I had to tell my story over and over again. Then, a revolving door of people came in and out of the room, grilling me and making me repeat the same details. They said they needed to be certain that the story was consistent, the facts unwavering. It was essential for me to prove that I was the winner and convince lottery officials that I did not steal this ticket from anyone else. That day became the first of more than 500 times I have told my story and I never tire of it.

The winning ticket was taken from me for verification. I was nervous to give it up. The word here is that I was having the fantods. The English language has a word for almost anything. "Fantods" is a great one, a 19th century term, possibly related, dictionaries say, to fantastic and fantasy and fatigue. It perfectly describes the weird state of nervous irritability that overtook me. I was told that the ticket was going to be put under an electron microscope to make sure that it was the real thing, not a copy or a fake. The ticket has precise imbedded microscopic imprints to show that it is genuine. Knowing I was a physician, the examiner let me view the ticket under the microscope. Each ticket has built-in unique markings of squiggly lines, different valleys and distinctive colors the naked eye cannot see.

We were told to go get lunch. Our lawyer regaled us with stories so the time passed more quickly. I was so wound up that I couldn't eat.

We went back to the offices and while waiting for the confirmation process to be completed, I was cold and shaking. I was afraid that it would turn out to be just a wishful dream. I envisioned a person coming out and saying, "Dr. Press, I'm sorry there's been a mistake and you are not the winner."

I kept saying to Bill, "Is this really happening?"

After some time, a man came out and led us to another room. He stated nonchalantly that my ticket was verified. That was it? My heart was pounding and that's all he said? Yes, that was it.

I was then given stacks of forms to fill out. I was told this was also needed for verification, but could not understand the necessity for so much legalese. This is proof positive why we needed to have an attorney with us.

I was given a choice of taking the winnings over a 20-year period or as a lump sum. The attorney recommended taking the immediate payout. He said if the state were ever to go bankrupt, it could theoretically default on the long-term payments of the winnings. The reality of that decision quickly took hold as the win was reduced to $28.8 million, approximately 50 percent of the total. Additionally, we had to pay 39 percent or $11.2 million of the reduced amount directly to the federal government in income taxes. And we were lucky to live in Florida, which does not have a state income tax.

After all this, the actual in-pocket amount of winnings came to $17.56 million. We basically received about 31 percent of the winning total. I was surprised, but who's complaining? It was still much more than my husband and I would ever earn over a lifetime.

Michael had already assembled what seemed to be an army of financial experts prepared to guide us through the process of setting up bank accounts and wiring the money into those accounts. Essentially, we became members of a private bank. As confusing as all of this was, I was in no position to argue. My head was spinning with all this new information. I remember my head throbbing probably from my migraine headaches or alternatively it could have been just stress. It was a whirlwind of data to absorb. I was feeling uneasy about it all.

Ironically, I came home from the lottery office with no money from the winnings. It takes days to access the money, so you leave with pretty much the same funds you had before the win. However, you are given a gigantic fake check as a souvenir.

As soon as I left, the state issued press releases on the radio, newspaper and television. I was informed that the press releases are mandatory in order to claim the winnings. There is the Sunshine Law in Florida, which effectively states that the agencies of the state must provide access to any person to view public records. The Florida Lotto is a business and the people running it urged me to do more publicity than the minimum required. I declined. They told me I was an atypical winner, being a physician, and I could encourage more professionals to buy tickets. I would have preferred no publicity at all because of privacy concerns. Due to September 11, the media's focus was probably reduced although *The Miami Herald* wrote a positive story about my winning the lottery. Of course, the horror of the Twin Towers tragedy overshadowed everything and rightfully so. Under normal circumstances, I appreciate publicity for accomplishments as much as the next guy but this was different. It was for a random, public event.

We hired two off-duty Miami Beach police officers to stay outside the house for the first few nights. I went back to work Monday, September 17 – and yes, I still work and never thought of quitting. Being a physician is part of my identity. The entire ER staff was all over me with congratulations and well wishes. For that one day, I felt like Bill Gates.

The doctor who stepped down from his position, came up to me and congratulated me. "You are a better poker player than I am," he said, for hiding the secret.

"Now don't you go getting that rich girl look," teased head ER nurse Gloria McSwain, a longtime friend and colleague, no doubt conjuring up a mental picture of plastic surgery and Botox.

Some people said it was God's will that I won because of the good I've done helping people, like the employee, whose daughter I saved by correctly diagnosing Kawasaki's Disease. (John Travolta's son was said to have suffered from this as well.) I do not agree. Far too many people do good work and don't hit the jackpot. If that was true, we would be a country filled with rich do-gooders and the bad guys would be poor.

There was a lot of reaction at the hospital and at home. Most of it was good and supportive. There were many congratulations, mazel tovs, emails, calls and cards. Even weeks and months later, people would come up to me and hug me. Some wanted my luck to rub off on them.

There was some jealousy as well, which can be expected. I can understand this. Some people said it wasn't fair that I won because I was already comfortable in life. This is true. Life isn't fair.

I, on the other hand, actually felt bad about feeling good at the time. This for me was mixed emotions – a familiar feeling. I kept thinking of the victims of Sept. 11 as well as other tragedies of life and here I was a newly cropped millionaire. Ambivalence is commonplace.

And there were lots and lots of solicitations. People came out of the woodwork selling all kinds of stuff like boats, cars, land deals, and oil wells. Stockbrokers promised incredible returns.

And there were troubling incidents as well. Two days after I returned to work, a man called the Pedi-ER. He asked if I was Dr. Press. I did not recognize the voice.

"Who are you?" I said.

"I'm going to get you," he threatened, then hung up.

I was taken back. Did that really happen? Yes. Am I in danger? Probably. I was in the public domain for that time. Needless to say, this really scared me. I was shaken.

Driving home one night, a couple of weeks later, my brakes failed. I thought I would crash. My husband told me to drive slowly and carefully to the house. Brian, our mechanic, discovered the next day that the brake lines had been tampered with. I hope randomly. I was frightened coming off the heels of the phone call. Again, I was shocked. The person may have wanted just to scare me but I could have been killed. I was put on guard.

Months passed without incident. I sifted through the offers. There were those looking to make a quick buck. Others were truly in need. One of our first requests for money came from Bill's Aunt Margie and Uncle Bobby. Their daughter Toby, Bill's first cousin, was fighting lymphoma and needed a stem cell transplant. She was a teacher in Austin, Texas and her health insurance denied coverage for this treatment, then considered experimental. Without a second thought, we immediately guaranteed the payment to the hospital. Tragically, Toby died a few days before the scheduled transplant. We were heartbroken. This was real life, not a made-for-TV movie.

Our priority remains giving first to family and friends. I have always believed in sharing, now more than ever. My list of favorite charities grows longer. It may be surprising, although not to my children, that I've yet to go on a wild spending spree. "Be sensible," I told myself. Sure, I've bought a few trinkets and stayed in deluxe hotels when I travel. However, frivolous spending is not in my nature. I often seek out sales when at the mall. I rarely leave a restaurant empty handed. It's the way I was raised. A life of luxury was pure fantasy. I know what it is to do without.

And I know the role luck plays in everyone's life. That was clear to me long before six numbers on a piece of paper changed my life forever.

.

2. Get Back

Fifty years before I ever heard of Quick Pick tickets or instant jackpots, I was born in Camden, N.J., the first child of Gershon and Leah Press.

I arrived at 8:42 p.m. on June 2, 1951. There is nothing remarkable about a 6 pound, 14 ounce baby girl, except that my very existence was a kind of miracle. My mother had survived Auschwitz, my father, Dachau. They met after both of them came separately to America. They married in 1948. They had defied the odds and now had the never easy job of raising a child. The next chapter describes a detailed account of their lives.

They rarely spoke of the Holocaust and chose not to burden my sister Barbara, born two and a half years later, and me with the past. They reserved speaking Yiddish, their native language, for private times, of which there were few. At the time, it all seemed so normal. Yet we instinctively understood the precious legacy of survivor children. My parents' priority was to bring up two assimilated girls in a free land and make a living the American way, yet never forgetting their Jewish heritage. It wasn't easy. My dad worked in the grocery store of his Aunt Rose and Uncle Morris Dworkin who sponsored his immigration to the United States after the war. Aunt Rose was my father's mother's sister.

My dad was a gentle, even-tempered soul. He always helped people. When he was in a position to do so, he would extend store credit to deserving customers. He would keep each family's tally on little pieces of white paper. He created an idiosyncratic way of filing these slips, storing them alphabetically on a series of six nails hammered into the wall in the store's backroom. At the end of each week, customers would come in and pay their tab. I remember him best in his white apron. He had a heavy accent. In addition, until the day he died, he had a full head of brown hair without a speck of gray. I inherited that trait from him. To this day, I have yet to see my first gray hair.

On only a grocer's salary, we could barely afford our first home, a tiny two bedroom one bath brick row house at 1494 Kenwood Avenue in Camden's Parkside section of town. They paid $8,000 for the house, which was on a typical city block. There was a small grocery store (not ours) on the corner, as well as a nearby synagogue. It was a five block walk to school. We knew many of our neighbors. Two blocks away lived our older cousins, Andrea, who we called Andy, and Mark Dworkin. Andrea grew up to find fame as a writer and feminist. However, as kids, it was Mark we sought out. We spent countless hours entertained by his bottle cap and baseball card collections. In the summer, we would also play in the Dworkins' inflatable swimming pool while our mothers would talk. I remember Andrea playing the piano, always reading, and talking with the adults. Later in life, we became close.

We always had enough to eat. My mother was a master at transforming hamburger into a variety of different dishes. She was also obsessed with eggs and thought giving us an egg a day would safeguard our health. Her original invention was to wait until she thought we weren't looking and quietly stir a raw egg into our Bosco Chocolate Syrup flavored milk. We weren't fooled, but dutifully drank the concoction to make her happy.

It was understood that I would wear hand-me-down clothes from cousins, and when I outgrew them, the cycle would continue with my younger sister. Afterwards, my mother would ship the clothes to our relatives in Israel for another rotation. We lived without air conditioning. The walls in our house were so thin that we were able to play knocking games from our respective bathtubs with our next-door neighbors, Keiran and Trevor Lynch.

My parents could not afford to buy a small black and white television set until 1956, and they purchased their first car, a green Ford Fairlane, in 1961, the year I turned 10. I had no expensive toys but will never forget Susan Serock's fancy dollhouse in her backyard across the street. Yet, tea parties at the dollhouse were far from my favorite pastime. There were no Barbies on my Hanukkah list. I preferred outdoor games like stickball, hopscotch and double-Dutch jump rope or playing in groups of kids that formed spontaneously. We'd play in an alley behind our house. I was usually accompanied by my cute little sister Barbara, who I had to drag with me pretty much everywhere. We shared a room and I still remember our matching plaid quilts. I never thought about whether we were rich or poor until Linda Hill, the only African-American girl on our block, enlightened me. "Look at the houses on the television and then look at ours," she would say.

The early years were good years, despite money woes. Our neighbor, Jim Serchia, became quite popular for his weekly nickel-and-dime giveaways. He was the original Alex Trebek of Kenwood Avenue, always asking the kids on the block questions about current affairs and rewarding us for right answers. We still keep in touch with "Uncle" Jim; in recent years he has become a close friend to my mother. It was typical of the 50s that we knew all our neighbors and rarely locked our doors. The only theft I was aware of was when someone stole my bicycle. It was later found up in the branches of an old oak tree. This was the extent of crime on Kenwood Avenue.

We were able to walk without fear each morning to Parkside School. Students were required to go home for lunch. While the other girls went home, I had to eat in the luncheonette section of the local five-and-ten cent store where my mother worked as a sales clerk. She was the only mother I knew who worked outside the home. The little money she made helped to make ends meet. My mother later arranged for Barb and me to eat at my classmate Ina Sirisky's house. I still keep in touch with her and other friends from the old neighborhood.

Along with regular school, I went to Beth El Hebrew School three times a week. Later on, I attended Hebrew High School followed by Midrashah Junior College, which was a continuation of Jewish education during eleventh and twelfth grades. There were no Bat Mitzvahs in the Conservative branch of Judaism at our synagogue. My mother, sister and I attended synagogue every Saturday. I never ate a piece of non-kosher meat until I went to college.

My best friend since third grade Marsha Rosenkrantz and I would walk to her apartment for milk and cookies before we went to Hebrew school. What I found odd was that her father was always home. I had noticed that his hands and head were always shaking a bit. Nevertheless, I didn't think anything of it. I was oblivious to the fact that he had

Parkinson's disease and was disabled. Her father died when we were 18. I remember being at her father's funeral, thinking how lucky I was that my father was alive and well.

We worked hard, did without, and never complained because we all lived with the shadow of the Holocaust. Barb and I were latchkey kids throughout elementary school. Our mother did not get home from work until 4 or 5 o'clock. My father was not there to tuck us into bed at night because he always had to work late. My mother later found work as an assistant nursery school teacher at the Jewish Community Center (JCC). This job came with a bonus that gave us four free weeks of day camp at Camp Hilltop, in Medford, N.J. She also at one point became president of our elementary school's PTA.

Later, Rabbi Isaac Furman, who was principal of the nearby Kellman Academy, plucked my mother from the JCC to become a full-fledged nursery school teacher with the stipulation that she take several college level courses after he hired her. Rabbi Furman, a survivor himself, knew my mother had a natural flair for working with young children and glossed over her lack of formal credentials, instinctively understanding how the Holocaust had brutally curtailed her education. While she may have lacked a full bachelor's degree, she proved to be the school's best nursery school teacher. Even today, people come up to her, comment on how much their kids loved her, and provide updates on those former students.

Our fortunes improved when I was in the sixth grade. My father finally became his own boss when Aunt Rose and Uncle Morris sold him the store for $15,000. It was paid off at $3,000 a year for five years with no interest. This was one of his goals in life to own his own business. So we moved to the Morgan Village section of Camden and lived in the two bedroom apartment above the store. Barbara and I still shared a bedroom.

Some of the kids in my new school thought my name was "Shirley Gershwin" confusing my dad's first name with the last name of the famous composer. Still, it was a step up for us. Barbara and I spent a lot of time hanging out in the grocery store. The only phone in the store was a pay phone. We had to vie with customers and our dad to snag it for even a few minutes. A nickel bought customers three minutes of talking time. However, the phone also doubled as my father's business line, on which he used to take orders.

After the allotted time was exhausted, I remember my father banging on the phone booth shouting to the customer, "Your time is up, don't put another nickel in!"

Soon, Barb and I were both part of the family business. By the seventh grade, I was put in charge of the cash register during the late afternoons and early evenings. My manning of the cash register gave my mother "a break" so that she could prepare dinner upstairs in the apartment. The store had three aisles of food, a delicatessen counter and a butcher shop. There was no free meat for us since we kept kosher, but the best nickel and penny candy in the world was "free." I remember indulging in my favorites; candy cigarettes, Wax Lips, Baby Ruths, Wax Bottles, Bazooka bubble gum and Bonomo's Turkish Taffy. There has never been a candy like Turkish Taffy. You had to smack it against a wall to crack it into little pieces. Then you had to chew it so hard it felt like your fillings were coming out. It was a good value though. It took hours to finish one bar. We were the envy of the neighborhood kids and I can still remember the taste of the penny candy.

The store is also where my coin collecting began. Each night I would sort through the change from the cash register in search of valuable pennies, nickels, dimes and quarters. My finds were preserved in the Whitman blue coin albums that I have to this day. This led to three other collections: stamps, silver certificate dollar bills and my favorite at the time, the Beatles cards. The fun of collecting is the chase. At night, my sister and I would sneak downstairs to the store and surreptitiously unwrap the new cellophane packages of Beatles cards, remove the cards that we needed for our collection and replace them with our duplicates. Needless to say, we had the best collection in the neighborhood.

When I was in charge of the cash register, I made a game out of adding the total of each purchase in my head. Since I was a math whiz, I usually beat out our old-fashioned NCR cash register. In addition, my dad found another way to keep a young girl interested in the store. He put me in charge of redeeming the customers' food coupons. Four times a year, I would gather all of the coupons that my parents had redeemed for the customers, sort them by manufacturer and submit them to each company for reimbursement. In those days, the mark-up for the grocer was 2 cents per coupon. Therefore, for a 5-cent coupon, I would receive 7 cents in the mail by check from the companies a few weeks later. Multiply this by hundreds of coupons and there was a hefty profit for that tedious work. I was ecstatic when the checks actually arrived in the mail. My father would let me keep the value of the coupons, so that was the big incentive to do the coupon work. Yes, I was the "coupon girl" back then.

We had a similar arrangement when it came to the glass soda bottles. When we lived above the store, my father and I filled the garage with the bottles redeemed by customers for two cents or a nickel, depending on the size of the bottle. Every afternoon I would schlep the bottles, six-pack by six-pack, from the store to the adjacent garage. This helped us turn a profit on the bottles. It may not seem like much now, but it left me with some jingle in my pocket. Pennies had power back then.

My parents worked hard and they expected the same for Barb and me. My father also had high standards for his customers. They respected him and it was returned. Ron Cornwall, whose sister I went to school with, wrote to me on Facebook relating the following:

"I recently told a little story on FB about your Dad and an event in my life. Please remember I was a small child when it happened. He caught me stealing a peach pie. A Tastykake Peach Pie to be specific. He didn't scold me and he was kind but forceful in his tone and told me. 'You don't have to steal! You can work for it.' He took me outside and showed me how to properly use a corn broom. Then he let me sweep his whole corner, which was pretty big, for the pie. Two lingering aspects are, peach pie is still my favorite, (I make my own and they are delicious) and I think of him kindly, almost anytime I have a broom in my hands. Lessons well learned. With a kind heart and a tender embrace, Ron Cornwall"

That was the kind of person my father was.

Homework often waited until late evening, but that didn't stop me from being an "A" student. We lived by a strict standard for working at home, at school and at my parents' store. The values of our Jewish heritage dictated our approach to life, which included a willingness to work hard, a reverence for learning and compassion for others.

By now, when summer came we were able to spend some carefree days along the Atlantic City Boardwalk. My mother, sister and I traveled there along with my Aunt Ruchel who we called "Tanti" and her children, our only first cousins, Philip and Beverly. We would stay at an old boarding house that we fondly named "Hotel Dropsie." It was quite a dump with no air conditioners or phone. It had a dark kitchen where my mother and aunt made every meal. Little Bev was seven years my junior. At night, we kids took salt air strolls on the boardwalk and sometimes we would lose her. However, in those days we didn't worry. Either, we would find her wandering, or the boardwalk patrol would help us out. They knew us by our names. Inevitably, we all would end up in the pinball arcades. That is where I honed my skills in pinball and Skee-Ball in the pre-slot machine days. To this day, I'm still a ringer when it comes to winning stuffed animals at carnival Skee-Ball games.

My only real vacation during my childhood was when my mother sent me to stay with my cousins, the Kalishes, in Queens, New York during the 1964-65 New York World's Fair. My cousin Wendy and I marched around the glorious fair for hours on end. I, as a sheltered girl, got her first glimpse of the outside world.

Those carefree summer days were quickly replaced by struggles at home. School days never ended at 3 p.m. Besides working at the store, I had babysitting jobs where I earned 50 cents per hour. Moreover, while there was not a lot of free time after class I also played the violin, joined the chess club and won the role of a cheerleader in a school play. But for the most part, I lived the life of a shy girl in a sheltered world. I felt I was unpopular. Confidence was not my strong suit. I never rebelled. I never ran away from home. It was pre-women's liberation and I recall being forced to wear leggings under dresses to school in the winter as no pants were allowed.

As I got older, the reality of poverty became more apparent. Never eating out. The rare exception was going to the Horn & Hardart Automat in downtown Camden once a year for lunch with my mother. (The thrill of putting the coins in the machine may have also forecasted my love for slot machines.) None of the wildly popular John Romain, Villager or Ladybug brands of clothes for Barb or me. A life with scarce resources is recalled in unique ways. I still remember the crushing disappointment of not having the $5 to see the Beatles when they played in Philadelphia in 1964. Years later, I would have a much more personal encounter with Paul McCartney.

I made up for that teenage angst by managing to scrape together the money to see the band Herman's Hermits with my best friend Marsha in Atlantic City at the Steel Pier, "An Amusement City at Sea," which it really was, in August 1965. The other main draw was the premiere of the Beatles' movie *Help*. Add in the allure of the Diving Horse -- a woman on a horse diving off a high platform into the tank below -- and you were getting some amazing triple feature. The Herman's Hermits show was packed. What I remember most is Marsha getting faint. Like the loyal friend I was, I went out with her for a glass of water. And we lost our place in what seemed to be a sea of teenagers.

Most Atlantic City memories are of fun times, like watching the final episode of the TV show *The Fugitive* on August 29, 1967, in the lobby of Teplitsky's Hotel, crowded with 200 other teens. When I return there, I often remember what's left of the old Boardwalk and hangouts though I now really visit for the casino action. Like me, Atlantic City has reinvented itself.

I always did well in school, forever hitting the books at Hatch Junior High, Camden High and then Cherry Hill High West, to where I transferred in the 11th grade after my parents were finally able to buy a real house. It was a typical suburban, three bedroom home with gray painted aluminum siding. Switching schools in 11th grade did not cause my grades to suffer. Since I no longer worked at the store, I was able to concentrate mainly on my schoolwork. In addition, in the Cherry Hill house, we could actually park the car in a garage free of soda bottles. For the first time, my sister and I had our own bedrooms.

In my later teens, I had my first taste of wealth. My friend Joan Herman would take me down the shore to her family's summerhouse in Ventnor, a town just south of Atlantic City. The home was a ten bedroom Victorian, just five houses from the beach. She fixed me up with her brother, Jimmy, which lasted only a short while, as teen romances are apt to do. Joan's closet door was open to me when it came time to discard last season's wardrobe. Joan's tragic death was an early example that money doesn't guarantee happiness. At the age of 23, Joan accidentally killed herself with carbon monoxide poisoning in the family garage. To this day, I am convinced she wanted to be found. I still see her parents from time to time.

But in my little world, I was figuring out how to get to college. I knew that my family could not afford to pay for a private school. Good grades and all that studying paid off with a full scholarship to New York University at the downtown campus.

Growing up "me" was no sitcom. Though there were wonderful times, we knew from our earliest years that life would be full of challenges and struggles. Even then, Camden was no place to brag about, though it was renowned for RCA and the Campbell's Soup Company. Now, it has the dubious distinction of often topping the "murder capital of the United States" charts.

As I got older, I escaped for hours into the happy households beamed into ours on our black-and-white Zenith television. I would be in college before my family could buy a color set. I lived in the shadow of the happy households of *Leave it to Beaver, The Donna Reed Show* and

Father Knows Best. True, my mother was no June Cleaver and my father bore no resemblance to Jim Anderson. However, they nurtured a fine family from the ashes of the Holocaust.

Nevertheless, one of my prime pet peeves is romanticizing being poor. We were poor. And it wasn't always fun. TV shows like *Good Times* and *The Waltons* pretend that it was fun. There is a lot that those shows don't reveal like the stress of parents working two jobs and children worried too early in life with how much money is coming in. No one had to teach me frugality. I lived it. Even as a young woman, I knew I was going to find a path to a better life one way or another. About the only good thing about growing up poor is that it gives you a lot of motivation to become rich.

3. The Long and Winding Road: My Parents and the Holocaust

My parents are both Holocaust survivors and I would feel remiss if I did not include their stories in my book. World War II ended in 1945, but it never really ended for my parents. Although they did not go through the war together and met here, in America, their common experiences drew them together in a way that only other survivors might understand. Fate or luck made them survivors when most others perished. Their lives are a part of my life and that of my sister.

In childhood, Barb and I realized our parents were different but we weren't quite sure how. When I was nine, a Hebrew schoolteacher taught us an age-appropriate history of the Holocaust. With this knowledge, the pieces started to fit together. My parents hadn't spoken much about their past. They wanted to make our lives as normal – as American – as possible.

Yet the Holocaust never really went away. Mom, when exasperated with our behavior, would sometimes remind us that she weighed about 70 pounds and was at death's door when she was liberated.

I don't know how many times while we were growing up she said, "When I was 15, I had already lost my parents and two sisters."

Therefore, Barb and I hid personal problems and did not tell her about things that were bothering us, for they paled in comparison to her life. For example, the kids at Hebrew school teased me relentlessly and I should have transferred to another school. She never knew because I kept my distress a secret. That's what the second generation did.

After I won the lottery, I had time to further explore my parents' lives. In 2005, Bill and I went on a trip to Central Europe sponsored by the Greater Miami Jewish Federation. We saw some of the concentration camps and visited cities and towns in Poland where Jewish life was once so vibrant. In Warsaw, we went to a functioning synagogue. Even so, it was a place where the past refused to stay silent. "Everyday Poles come to me saying, 'I think I'm Jewish and I want to learn about Judaism,' " the rabbi told us.

After Warsaw, we traveled to Krakow where the main synagogue had been turned into a museum; there are no more Jews left to use it. Our trip continued to the concentration camps. We then visited Auschwitz. It was terrible. Auschwitz looked so serene, with attractive, red brick buildings on the outside that belied the atrocities that occurred within its walls. The site of the crematorium brought tears to my eyes. It ripped me to pieces to know that my mother and aunt had been tortured there.

A researcher at the Auschwitz library was able to find just one piece of information about my mother, from a camp log dated August 11, 1944. Translated into English, it stated, "1,999 female Jews who are selected from the transit camp in Birkenau receive Nos. A-21001 - A-22999. There are probably Hungarians and Poles among them." There was the number that had been tattooed onto my mother's left arm, A-

21653 in that grouping – absolute proof that she had been there and the Holocaust existed. Birkenau is also known as "Auschwitz II – Birkenau" an extermination camp three kilometers from the original Auschwitz camp. The librarian suggested that I contact the International Tracing Service (ITS) in Bad Arolsen, Germany for more information. The ITS is an internationally governed archive which houses 50 million records about the 17.5 million victims of Nazi persecution, including Jews, homosexuals, Gypsies, the handicapped and other "undesirables." and has been affiliated with the International Commission of the Red Cross. Most of its records can now be requested online.

Shoah is the Hebrew word for "calamity," or "catastrophe," and its use is now mostly reserved for the Holocaust. The push to gather testimony from survivors didn't really get underway until the 80s and 90s, long after my dad had passed away. Had my father lived, I am certain he would have also given his testimony to the Shoah Foundation, now under the auspices of the University of Southern California.

When I started writing this book, I continued to research my parents' experiences during the Holocaust. For my father's history, I had to rely on documents from the ITS, the United States Holocaust Memorial Museum, and HIAS (Hebrew Immigrant Aid Society.) I also interviewed family and friends. According to ITS records, Gershon Press was born on June 14, 1918, in the Lithuanian town of Kovno. There are no records of my father's parents Beines and Sonja (nee Cohn) or his younger brothers Beryl, and twins Meyer and Welrel. The only recollection I have of my grandfather that my father told us was that he had been drafted into the Russian army during World War I. My father also had told us that he was really born in 1921 and that his official records were wrong. Sam Sherron who had been a childhood friend of my father's brother Beryl confirmed this. Sam had also been in the Kovno ghetto with my father. They were reunited at the Feldafing DP (displaced persons) camp in 1945 after both had been in concentration camps. Afterward, they found each other again in America and grew close. When I interviewed Sam in 2010 at age 84, he specifically remembered that my father had been five years older than him. Despite the horrors of the Holocaust, Sam insisted that my father survived to live the life of "a happy person."

Another person who knows about my father's past and remembers him very well is our former neighbor, Jim Serchia – the one who gave us kids nickels and dimes for answering his current affairs questions correctly. He and my dad were best friends. Jim said that Gershon had to shoulder a lot of family responsibility after his father died early from a stroke.

"He had to become the breadwinner," Jim said.

Another fact Jim recalled was that sometime during my father's early childhood his family moved to Sveksna, Lithuania, not far from the Baltic Sea. The earliest documentation of this town is in the 14th century according to *Sveksna: Our Town* by Esther Herschman Rechtschafner. She wrote a Jewish history of the town that is available online at http://kehilalinks.jewishgen.org/sveksna/. According to Rechtschafner's research, Jews had a rich past in Sveksna. The Jewish community dates back from at least the 17th century and was the site of an important Yeshiva renowned for its brilliant scholars. There was also plenty of anti-Semitism, which lasted well into the 20th century. As late as the mid-1930s, a rabbi was accused of killing a Christian boy to use his blood to make matzoh.

At the time of the 1941 German invasion, my father was living and working in Kovno, which is not far from Sveksna. His job was shearing the skin off cattle and curing it into shoe leather. His mother and younger brothers had stayed behind in Sveksna. The Nazis captured them and murdered them with machine guns, part of the Germans' large-scale immediate slaughter of the Jews. They were buried in ditches in a mass grave in Inkakliai, Lithuania, in September of 1941.

My father was arrested on August 15, 1941, at the age of 20, and was confined in Kovno's ghetto where he endured forced labor. In 1943, it was converted to the Kovno concentration camp where he became a slave laborer. On July 29, 1944, he was transferred to Dachau concentration camp in Germany where he was assigned the number 84847. According to the reference book *Hidden History of the Kovno Ghetto* published by the United States Holocaust Memorial Museum, out of a total of 235,000 Jews living in Lithuania before the war, only a few thousand survived.

My father told my sister and me that he was a baker inside the camp making bread for the German soldiers. As a result, he was able to hide bread for himself and his friends. On one of his official documents, his profession was listed as weaver. As Barb and I were growing up, we saw no evidence of either trade in his life. He never ever cooked. He never sewed – with one exception; I remember that my father accidently sliced off the edge of his thumb when chopping meat in our grocery store. He calmly and without anesthetic sutured it back together with a needle and thread. He saw a doctor the next day who said he did a fine job. Perhaps, he really did know how to sew.

Our former neighbor and friend Jim related this story about our father saying, "He said he was running away from the Germans during the war and eventually got caught. He said he was fortunate to have been assigned to a German officer and became more or less a valet. He would do chores for him." My father also told Jim that he remembered the officer as being decent and that he had enough to eat.

My father was liberated from Dachau by the United States Army on April 29, 1945. According to ITS records, he was registered in the DP camp known as Feldafing on October10, 1945. He also spent time in the Landsberg DP camp, the largest such camp in Europe. In my research, I came across Colonel Irving Heymont's description of the camp in *Generations*, the United States Holocaust Memorial Museum's newsletter, the Fall 2009 edition.

"The camp is filthy beyond description. Sanitation is virtually unknown," he wrote in September 1945. "Words fail me when I try to think of an adequate description. The people of the camp themselves appear demoralized beyond hope of rehabilitation. They appear to be beaten both spiritually and physically, with no hopes or incentives for the future..." The colonel underestimated the resolve of people like my parents and other survivors.

On May 10, 1946, according to the passenger manifest form, my father boarded the "SS Marine Flasher" which sailed from Bremen, Germany. The fare was $142, the equivalent of $1693 in 2013. HIAS and my father's Uncle Morris and Aunt Rose assisted my father in leaving his devastated life in Europe. He landed in New York on May 20, 1946.

His first cousin Betty Dworkin Ettinger vividly remembers that date because her marriage to Sig Ettinger took place one day earlier in Philadelphia. They were on their honeymoon 90 miles north in New York City. Her father, Uncle Morris Dworkin, knocked on her hotel room door.

"What are you doing here?" she asked in total shock.

"I'm here to pick up your first cousin Gershon who survived the war," he replied.

When he arrived in America, my father was fluent in Yiddish, Lithuanian, Italian, German and English. Betty and her brother Leon told me that my father spoke English well when he arrived in the United States. According to his friend Sam, they both learned English in Feldafing DP camp where classes were given to help the refugees with their eventual resettlement.

Aunt Rose was my father's mother's sister. She and her siblings grew up in Vitebsk, Belarus, which is the birthplace of the artist Marc Chagall. Rose fell in love with a Lithuanian dreamer named Morris Dworkin, born in 1894, who immigrated to America at 19 to find a better life. He sent for Rose to join him and they married in the United States in 1914 and settled in Camden. They had three children Harry, Leon and Betty.

After arriving in the United States, my dad went to live with his aunt and uncle in the apartment above Morris's grocery store on Fairview Street in Camden. Cousin Leon, who was a WWII veteran, shared a room with my father -- the same bedroom my sister and I shared many years later. Cousin Harry, also a vet, had married and was living elsewhere in Camden. According to Leon, my father was a good-natured man who "fit in nicely" and "adapted well to this country." He said to me, "Your father felt more like a brother than a cousin." The time they spent together at home and at the family store left Leon with the impression that my father was not bitter about what had happened to him. Cousin Betty also felt that my father was not a bitter man.

According to records at HIAS, my father secured employment in August of 1946 at the Phillipsburg Textile Print Works, Inc. in Philadelphia and earned $34 ($405 equivalent in 2013) a week. He was also attending night school to further his knowledge of English. My father's caseworker at the Jewish Federation of Camden County in New Jersey wrote an evaluation in November, 1946, stating, "He has made an excellent adjustment."

Jim Serchia also described my father as a man with a big heart who had a knack for making friends and was open with everyone. In Jim's words, "When he had that grocery store, if someone said, 'Gershon, could I have an apple?' he would say 'take the apple'. He had a heart of gold. He was very happy to have survived the things that went on in Europe, very happy that his aunt and uncle sponsored him. I don't recall him ever complaining or saying anything derogatory."

He said that my father was willing to discuss the war years with him, perhaps because Jim had his own memories of Europe. He had served with the 38th Mechanized Cavalry and landed on Omaha Beach six days after the initial Allied invasion. Jim said that his unit went through France, Belgium and Germany and he witnessed the horror of the concentration camps.

Sol Zytcer, another friend, met my father two years after his arrival in America. He spoke about my father's job switch from a 75 cent per hour presser in the textile factory to working in a shoe leather factory, which paid more. The latter job lasted only two days because Uncle Morris needed him to work in the grocery store. Sol labeled my father "a lovable man" who would sneak over to his house to eat schmaltz herring, butter and rye bread. Those foods were against his doctor's orders because of his sky-high cholesterol. When speaking to Sol's children, Faye and Bobby, both have vivid memories of their mother Molly serving my father the schmaltz herring and butter.

Sol also remembers the night my parents met. It was at a meeting in 1948 in Philadelphia at the Bellevue-Stratford Hotel where Moshe

Sharett, the first Minister of Foreign Affairs from Israel, was speaking. My father, I assume, went because of his passion for history - especially Russian and Jewish history. Dad was talking too loudly; my mother turned around and told him to be quiet. As they say, this was the beginning of a beautiful romance.

Another family friend Frieda Levy described my father as "the kindest person always giving rides to people."

"He just smiled all the time," my mother said. They were married on December 18, 1948, and were together until he died.

My father was the one waiting at New York Harbor to meet my Aunt Ruchel and her husband, my Uncle Herbert "Hashel" Kirschner, who she met and married in a DP camp, when they arrived in America on December 17, 1949. Uncle Hashel also recalls my father's down-to-earth nature. "He was a nice, nice man," he said, "who never thought of himself as a big shot."

Sadly, after overcoming extreme adversity during WWII, it was an incident in America that finally took its toll on my father. Robbers came to the grocery store and locked my father in the meat storage locker at gun point. He almost froze to death. I always felt that this incident contributed to his death, just a few months later, on March 30, 1970. His friend Sol believes that it changed Gershon since he seemed "more depressed and less trusting" after the attack. My father's tragic early death from a massive stroke meant that he missed out on so much in life especially knowing his five grandchildren.

I have been in contact with the United States Holocaust Memorial Museum, which also gave me information on my father. I sent Ms. Judy Cohen, Director, Photographic Reference Collection at the museum, photos of my father and his family before the war and they are now part of the museum's archives. I also posted photos of my father and his family at http://kehilalinks.jewishgen.org/sveksna/Press_Family.html. and wrote about my father's life story on HIAS's website at http://mystory.hias.org/en/stories/view/index/identity/1302.

As far as telling the story of my mother's life, I have more information on her experience in Europe. Not only have I been able to talk to her but I also have the ITS research and five hours on tape of her being interviewed about her life. My mother's only surviving sister, Ruchel Kirschner (Aunt Ruchel), also recorded her story for the Shoah Foundation. We also have video recordings of my mother talking at New Jersey schools and noting how it felt like a lifetime and a world away from Čierny Potok, Czechoslovakia where my mother grew up with her three sisters Ruchel, Bluma and Malka, and her parents, Sheindel and Eli Grünberg.

Though the ITS has documents relating to my mother and Aunt Ruchel (and nothing about my grandparents or Bluma and Malka), it's my mother's tapes that bring the era to life in a way no document ever could.

She was born Lenke Grünberg on September 14, 1929, the second oldest of Eli (aka Illes) Grünberg and Sheindel (aka Zseni) Schwimmer Grünberg in Čierny Potok, close to the Carpathian Mountains. Her father was a businessman who owned a farm and maybe a mill. He was an orphan. My mother remembers Čierny Potok as an idyllic small town where everyone knew each other.

"If there was a Gentile wedding, a Jewish wedding, everybody was there, whether you were invited or not," she said. "There was no place I would rather be."

My mother and her sister adored their mother, Sheindel. "I thought nobody in this world had such a mother as we did," she said, remembering her as a gentle woman who never raised her voice.

Townspeople would ask Sheindel to write letters for them, and my mother remembers her reading the Bible to the girls on Shabbat. "If mother would drop something, all of us would run to pick it up," she said. "I would rather be with her than any of my friends."

The nightmare of her life began at age 14, on April 9, 1944, the second day of Passover. At that time, the Hungarians, who were in collaboration with the Germans, controlled the town. Policemen warned the town's few Jews against celebrating Passover, but the family went ahead. My mother, in the tape, said it was a very different Passover from the usual happy occasion; tense and frightening.

"The worst part was when I saw tears streaming down his (her father's) face. I knew something was very wrong," she said. "I never saw him cry before that time. He knew it would probably be our last Passover."

The next day the police forcibly removed them from their modest home and sent them to the Mukačevo ghetto in Hungary. In 1945, Mukačevo became part of the Ukraine. "Dad said 'take food; make sure you are taking food.' "

Mukačevo is the name in Czech and Slovakian. Other names for this town are Munkács in Hungarian, Munkatsch in German (and Munkatch in Yiddish), evidence of how the ruling authority was always changing in that part of the world.

When asked by the Shoah Foundation interviewer what languages she spoke, my mother replied, "We spoke Yiddish, Ukrainian, German, Hungarian, truly, I don't think we learned any language perfectly."

On May 11, 1944, after a month in Mukačevo, they were transported to Auschwitz by rail in a locked cattle car crammed wall-to-wall.

"We had no idea where we were going," my mother recalls. "I remember looking through this tiny window (in the cattle car) and seeing the green grass and thinking, 'how beautiful the world is, but not for us.' It was the second time I saw my father cry."

At the camp, those assigned to the right were selected for work, at least temporarily. People deemed too old, young, feeble or too weak to work were assigned to the left and slaughtered. Her parents and sister Malka, the youngest at age 8, were murdered in the gas chambers right after their arrival.

"We arrived at night," my mother said. "No matter how eloquent a person is, there is no way to express the feeling on arrival to Auschwitz."

"They took away the most precious thing in my life, my mother – she was only 42 years old – and my precious sister Malka," my mother said.

My mother and her sisters, Ruchel and Bluma, were sent to the barracks after their heads were shaved, the first step in the dehumanization process.

"My sister was right in front of me and I didn't recognize her," my mother said.

No one could escape the sight of flames and smell of smoke coming from the crematoria. My mother remembers her shock when she first encountered the emaciated, hollow-eyed children in the barracks. When the other girls in the barracks told her and her sisters that their parents and Malka were almost certainly already up in smoke, my mother recalls how "We just cried and cried and cried."

At Auschwitz, survival was the only goal. My mother, Ruchel and Bluma were assigned to digging ditches. "We gave each other some kind of hope; we will get out of here, we will make it. They could never take away from me my will to live and my faith in God, though I was very angry with God," she said.

Every day meant standing in formation for hours. Every day there was a selection. They always took somebody. Each morning my mother and her sisters would pinch their cheeks to look healthy enough to work though they were being starved and the hunger was constant. Each day they would be given soup, one piece of black bread and a little butter.

"It's the kind of hunger that there is nothing in this world you would not give for a piece of bread," my mother said. One day, she impulsively ran out of the barracks door with her food container when she saw the people with the soup cauldron approaching. She was lucky not to have been beaten to death then and there. She was forced to kneel for hours on gravel.

A few weeks later, they were moved to Plaszow, the concentration camp portrayed in *Schindler's List*. This camp was actually worse than Auschwitz. Lice were rampant. They labored 12 hours a day hauling stones. There were savage, unpredictable shootings and beatings. German shepherds dogged their heels, ready to attack if someone fell.

Sadly, Bluma, my mother's younger sister was weakening. To try to conserve energy, the sisters would try and hide a piece of bread from their rations to eat later. One day, when the sisters were looking for the stash, they discovered it was gone. A girl came crying to them, "I took it," she sobbed. They all began crying. "Imagine, four kids crying over one piece of bread," said my mother.

Then in August 1944, they were transported back to Auschwitz. On August 11, 1944, the number, A-21653 was tattooed on her left arm. After arrival, there was another selection. It was overseen by Dr. Joseph Mengele, the infamous Nazi "Angel of Death." And the worst happened.

Bluma was selected.

"With one nod, they took Bluma up," my mother remembers. "Bluma screamed to us 'please don't let me go.' "

Ruchel tried to intercede, begging Mengele to let Bluma go. According to a tape made by Ruchel, he said to her, "Go back in line because you will die like a dog too."

My mother said she doesn't know if Bluma died from being clubbed right in front of them, or went to the gas chambers. "Many times I still hear her screams at night."

After that incident, it was getting harder to keep going. "Once our sister left us, our life was absolutely ruined, hope was diminishing," she said.

In the fall of 1944, my mother and her sister Ruchel were transferred to Bergen-Belsen. She said the stench of the dead bodies was awful. After Bergen-Belsen, their last camp was Buchenwald, which she and Ruchel entered December 17, 1944. For the final months, my mother was placed in a subcamp called Markkleeberg.

Finally, with the Allies invading from all sides, my mother, her sister and about 2,000 others were sent on a death march to Theresienstadt in northern Czechoslovakia. Fewer than 200 would survive. It was during the march that my mother escaped. They were forced to walk nonstop, with just an hour or so of sleep each night. They were given a piece of bread at the beginning of each day, then nothing. After about two weeks, my mother saw a field of freshly planted potatoes. On impulse, the same kind of impulse that sent her out for extra soup, she darted into the field.

"There I go again," she said. "I'm thinking, 'I'm just going to dig up the plants and come right back.' " But she fainted and when she came to, the others were gone. "I woke up and there were three potatoes and no one but God was with me. Those three potatoes were the best food I ever had."

My mother soon met up with two other death march escapees. She told us that upon liberation, she weighed approximately 70 pounds and she is 5 feet 3 inches tall. She just began walking and walking.

After the war, my mother learned that Ruchel had made it alive to Theresienstadt. Eventually, they reunited in Čierny Potok, their hometown. When they returned to the town, they found that their house had been turned into a small school. They were given a room, but it was clear there was no future there. "At that time I was very surprised the people in the town were not happy to see us," my mother said.

She went to work in Prague as a babysitter and then worked in a bakery. In 1946 she and her sister were placed in a series of displaced persons camps through the Joint Distribution Committee. At first, in the DP camps, people talked about their experiences. Then they stopped.

"We had the incentive to build a new life, the incentive to work hard, not hating people," she said

The last DP camp was DP Camp Deggendorf in Germany. My mother described this as "heaven" compared to the concentration camps. The survivors were given plenty of food and my mother described herself as a "blimp" for that period of her life. She had her own cot. In the camp there were also cultural and social events and schooling. My mother attended the dressmaking school sponsored by ORT, the Jewish educational and vocational training organization. She remembered going to lectures on Zionism and joined the Betar Movement which was a Zionist youth organization for a while. There was a makeshift synagogue and medical facilities. Life moved forward for many as there were many marriages and babies born there. My Aunt Ruchel married her husband

Hashel there in a hand-me-down wedding gown.

My mother was able to obtain a "child's visa" and immigrated to the United States alone. HIAS also participated in this process. She began her journey to the United States on October 15, 1947, also at the port of Bremen, Germany aboard the "Ernie Pyle." When my mother arrived in New York, her name was Lenke. She changed it to Leah shortly thereafter. Her American relatives, who were her sponsors, Uncle Louis and Aunt Zina Schwimmer, met her in New York. Uncle Louis was my grandmother's brother who immigrated to the United States in 1912 when he was 19 years old. She went to live with them and their daughter Dorothy Schwimmer, Mom's first cousin. She lived with them in Philadelphia where her aunt and uncle owned a grocery store. My mother went to work in a factory and took classes at night at the local high school. My mother had three other first cousins and she embraced her American relatives. Her mother Sheindel had another brother Jacob (Jake) Schwimmer who also left Europe before the war. Jake married Katie and had three children Seymour, Irving and Evelyn. According to my second cousins Peter Schwimmer (Seymour and Ruthie's son) and Robert Kalish (Evelyn and Philip's son) Jake was quite a colorful character. He earned his living by rolling cigars in his shop in the Bronx but his real zeal in life was hustling poker and pinochle games. According to an audio tape interview recorded by Robert Kalish in 1962, Uncle Jake was a self-ascribed gambler often becoming broke in the process. Mom became close with her cousins Seymour, a professor at Bloomsburg University in Pennsylvania, his wife Ruthie, a middle school teacher, and Evelyn and her husband Philip Kalish. She was also very close with another cousin Dorothy Shatoff. My family got together with them and their children throughout our childhood.

Each of my parents dealt in their own way with the tragedy of losing their families and being tortured in the concentration camps. Both were motivated to begin anew in America. They insisted on learning proper English and rarely spoke the other languages they knew. I wish that they had taught us Yiddish. My mother worked hard to speak unaccented English. I thought her English was perfect yet people always asked where my mother was from so I guess she had a slight accent after all. My father and mother each came here with nothing. Just surviving was a miracle. To assimilate as well as they did, make a living and raise two successful daughters was very hard and quite an achievement.

Having children helped them adjust to their post-war lives. We were proof of their existence and gave them a future. I was named Shirley in memory of my grandmothers, Sheindel and Sonja. Barbara was named for our grandfathers Bienes and Eli – Barbara Ellen. I have no middle name.

Still, my mother was very much aware of how the Holocaust affected her and others.

"Without freedom," my mother said, "the inner soul is taken away."

I am not certain if she ever got back all of hers. She was sometimes depressed, especially on the Yahrzeit - the dates of the death – of her parents and sisters.

And the past had a way of unexpectedly sneaking back. In the Shoah tape, my mother tells of how the 1995 Oklahoma City bombing brought back so much pain, especially when one newscast showed a little child's abandoned sneaker.

"I went hysterical," she said. "How many little sneakers did I see? How many little shoes? I cried for a whole week."

For years, neither of my parents spoke openly about their experiences.

My mother would only explain her tattoo to other adults, never to children. She was forever bitter toward Germans. Products made there, no matter the quality, were not permitted in our home.

It is not surprising that my mother gravitated to life's underdogs. She would always help others, even those who took advantage of her. She never forgot what it was like to do without and ridiculously deprived herself of good food, eating only cottage cheese or chicken for days on end. It made her feel safe to save money.

Considering her experience coming close to starving to death, food took on the utmost importance in our house. She forced my sister and me to eat way beyond what was normal. It's amazing that we were never even close to fat.

My parents mostly associated with other Holocaust survivors. For decades, they referred to themselves as "greena," because they were so "green" as in greenhorns, when they arrived in America.

In later years, there seemed to be a tacit hierarchy or pecking order that developed among Holocaust survivors. Some who survived the camps felt that their experiences really were more devastating than those who were hidden during the war years, passed as Gentiles or lived in the forests.

After my father died in 1970, my mother eventually remarried and was widowed again. In the 80s after she retired, my mother began speaking about the Holocaust to New Jersey school children, for which she was given an award by former New Jersey Governor James McGreevey. Twice she told her story on tape, once for the Jewish Community Relations Council of Southern New Jersey in 1981 and another time in 1998 for the Survivors of the Shoah Visual History Foundation established by director Steven Spielberg after he made

Schindler's List.

"If I only make a tiny dent...there are so many (Holocaust) deniers now...I want them to know it did exist. Where there is indifference, try to be there, try not to be a bystander," she said.

The Shoah Institute interviewer asked my mother if there is anything she would like to tell her own children, and this is what she said: "I hope they remember their heritage. I hope they remember they came from Holocaust parents who loved them more than life. I hope they will be the kind of people that they have been, up until now, that they will instill the basic human kindness to the rest of their future families and just be together whenever they can. If there is a misunderstanding, not to worry about that, and keep families together and just be good people."

Well said, Mom.

4. Getting Better

I entered New York University in the fall of 1969. You traversed the Lincoln Tunnel and headed downtown. Manhattan is only 90 miles from where I grew up. It really wasn't that far. However, my family never thought of visiting the city while we were growing up.

I had only been to Manhattan once, on a brief Hebrew School confirmation trip to see some of the city's Jewish sites. So with one vinyl suitcase and a manual typewriter in hand, I boarded a Trailways bus. College seemed like it was a world away. When I think of what I brought to college, compared to the trunk full of boxes and digital equipment my daughter Sarah transported to school 33 years later, the contrast is striking.

Nevertheless, I took along a burning desire to live and learn; and that was more than enough. At first, I was overwhelmed by the sophistication of a big city. I did not mind the noise or the crowds. New York was an adventure. I immediately got caught up in the whirlwind and went with the flow.

Classes seemed secondary, although I made certain to keep up my grades. Math was my major. Yet, I found time to sample the drug culture that dominated the turbulent late 60s. I smoked marijuana and hashish for the first time; however, I did not care for either and chose the straight life. College is a time to experiment. I am glad I satisfied my curiosity.

I lived on University Place in Weinstein Hall, a brick high-rise in the center of the urban campus. One building housed men, the other "co-eds" which is what women college students were called at the time. College also meant living with strangers. One might think sharing a room with my sister for most of my life would have made having a roommate easy. Not the case. I never bonded with any of them. No loss there. However, I did find other friends in the dorm.

During my freshman year, I managed to keep myself quite busy. Political activism was sweeping across the nation's college campuses, including NYU. I was caught up as well. In November of 1969, I marched on Washington, D.C., with 500,000 others to protest the US involvement in the Vietnam War – The Moratorium to End the War in Vietnam. We traveled on buses. Those who organized this event did an amazing job. It was accomplished through old-fashioned networking. No computers, cell phones, faxes, email, texting, instant messaging, Facebook or Twitter. We college students, though disruptive and oft-times unruly, had our say. As a generation, we have the satisfaction of knowing that we changed history.

I do not like being as old as I am now, but I do like reminiscing about how cool we were back then. I even kept some of my clothing from that era, including fringed vests and bell-bottoms. On rare occasions, I have the chutzpah or guts to publicly wear one of my outfits, now considered vintage apparel.

During my second semester, I took a seminar in logic. A blond-haired, blue-eyed guy named Frank Greco sat next to me. We clicked. He was a pre-med student from Chicago. He became my first love. A few months after we met we became intimate. I lost my virginity without regret.

But tragedy struck when I went home for spring break. At 11:30 p.m. on Friday, March 27, 1970, I told my father that I was going downstairs to watch *The Tonight Show* and would be back to say good night after Johnny Carson's monologue. Several minutes later, I found my father passed out on the floor upstairs. He looked dead. I screamed for my mother who called an ambulance. Sadly, it was too late. Daddy had suffered a major stroke and never regained consciousness. He died three days later in intensive care. He was only 48, and my mother was only 40. This was three weeks after my friend Marsha's father died.

His premature death left me numb. During the week of Jewish mourning called "shivah," I did not allow my boyfriend to visit because he was not Jewish. This would have only further upset my mother.

My father's death marked my very first loss of a family member. I was totally devastated and in shock. I cried all the time. While losing a grandparent can be a sad, even traumatic, event in the lives of many children, Holocaust survivor children rarely had grandparents since most were murdered in the concentration camps. On one occasion when I was young, I did ask my mother why we didn't have any grandparents. She just went upstairs and cried. I never asked again.

We didn't have grandparents in our lives to enrich and spoil us or be our fan in life. This also meant we didn't learn about death in a more natural progression, with elderly grandparents passing on first. Our families were small. My only experience as a granddaughter occurred a few years ago when I filled out an International Tracing Service form to try to find records of my grandparents' lives as I attempted to piece together my family history.

At that point in my life, I selfishly thought mostly of myself, and my loss. On reflection, I realized how terribly more tragic it was for my mother who had lost of both of her parents and two sisters during the war. Her life was scarred. My father's death had left her only the store, which for financial reasons, she was forced to sell.

My dad had not qualified for life insurance because of his sky-high cholesterol and a previous stroke. When my sister left for college two years later, my mother was all alone as a widow, though she later remarried.

I returned to the city two weeks after my dad died. Frank had asked me about the bus I planned to take back to school. Going up the escalator in the immense Port Authority station, I saw Frank waiting for me at the top. In today's world it is no big deal with the advent of the cell phone, but back then I felt that this was the nicest thing someone could have done for me. I was so depressed and weeks behind on schoolwork. With diligence, I managed to catch up through my tears. I had a hard time coming to terms with the finality of death. When I called home from college, I'd almost expect to talk to my father and then it would hit me again.

That summer Frank and I decided to travel to Europe. My mother thought I would be going with a girlfriend. To save for the trip, I worked in a bank verifying customer checks through June and July. I was known as a check checker. It was my first time on an airplane. I went to London, where I stayed at a youth hostel. Frank was already in Grenoble, France, where he had enrolled in classes. We planned to meet later in Paris.

This is where the other incredible event of my life, along with winning the lottery, took place. I participated in an amazing adventure, so out of character for me. If I didn't have the photos, I wouldn't believe it actually occurred. Simply put, I, at the age of 19, broke into Paul McCartney's house on Cavendish Avenue, St John's Wood, London NW8.

There, I said it. It's a confession that until now, I've only shared with family and a handful of close friends. I was just a kid at the time who wanted to have fun and I saw a chance to do something so beyond my sensible self. So when the plan's masterminds asked me to join in on this caper, I simply could not refuse.

Here's what happened. It was August 10, 1970. I was spending my days exploring the city's sites and soaking in the London street scene, still crowded with women wearing mod design clothes and hippies with backpacks. Though I was on my own for that part of my summer journey, there were so many kids anxious to see the city that I never truly felt alone. The day before the adventure, three guys staying in my hostel were boasting about their big escapade. They claimed that they had climbed over the stone wall of Paul McCartney's house and found an unlocked basement door. They had explored the home, then left. They said they stole nothing. They had not even taken a camera with them or had proof of the break-in. They were just proud to have been able to walk the halls of Paul's home and get out unscathed.

A few of us teased them and told them that we did not believe a word they said. However, the guys readily volunteered to return and asked me if I wanted to come along. I, being a huge Beatles fan, of course immediately said yes. Fleeting thoughts of being arrested, put in jail and losing my scholarship came to mind but then passed. Instead, I instantly flashed back to the missed opportunity of seeing the Beatles' Philadelphia concert. If these boys were telling the truth, this was my chance to one-up all of the screaming fans who were at that concert.

The next evening around dusk, the four of us ventured out. I, the featherweight at 100 pounds, was hoisted over the wall and told to check if the door was still unlocked. I dutifully discovered that it was indeed unlocked and signaled for the three others to follow. No dogs leaped out at us and no alarms went off.

We entered a world that was definitely different from the one we were all living in. The house was a mini palace. It was grand. It was like a fantasy, and this time we had a camera. The rooms were unpretentious and magnificent all at the same time. As spectacular as it was, there was also a sense of simplicity to it, as if one could tell that Paul never flaunted his wealth with material things that were not important to his life.

The paintings on the walls, along with the pictures scattered throughout, showed a family man, a man of simple taste, and one who enjoyed the beauty of life. We had a sense of pride in ourselves as we walked through all of the rooms, knowing that this larger-than-life man in public was something else in private. He seemed to be a regular "bloke" and never went overboard with his fame and fortune. In fact, all of us developed an even greater respect for him than we could have ever imagined.

We took as many photos of ourselves in the house as we could and made a pact not to move anything out of the way. It was eerie at times walking through this compact city mansion. As quiet as it was, we were all too afraid to make a single sound, just in case anyone was waiting outside to detain the novice intruders. The only noise made was when one of the boys accidently tripped on a loose carpet in the bedroom. His grunt as he landed caused us all to laugh, but then we quickly "shushed" each other like the amateur "criminals" we were.

I walked where Paul walked, went into his rooms and saw all of his awards, photos and memorabilia. Blundering our way from room to room frantically, we took a few photos for ourselves and these in turn became proof that we were really there. There is one where we are in Paul's sitar room and I'm holding his guitar. There is another one of us holding photos of the Beatles. And finally, there's one where I'm sitting beside a big *Sgt. Pepper's Lonely Hearts Club Band* medallion hanging on the wall. These are posted on my website www.shirleypress.com. The others with me in the photos were Lewis Spatts from Marblehead, Mass., and two college students from France. It was glorious. It was an adrenaline rush. We were so scared. My heart was racing and I had the shakes the whole time. I believe we were there for approximately 30 minutes and exited as fast as we entered. I have often tried to find my partners in crime through Google and Facebook but to no avail.

We snuck out the way we came in, through the basement door, over the wall and back into the night. My break-in to Paul McCartney's house qualifies as the absolute most stupid event of my life. I do apologize, Sir Paul. Please do not hold this against me all these years later.

From this crazy adventure, I understood why taking photos is vital. It's proof. If I didn't have the photos of myself in the house, it could have seemed to others to have been a fantasy, a flight of my imagination, or even a dream. Even as I tell the story and look at the 40 year old photos, it still sounds implausible.

I've often thought of the coincidence or luck of being in just the right place at the right time to take part in this nighttime feat. Thoughts of my teen adventure returned to me after I won the lottery. Memories of how

Paul seemed to live with both wealth and graciousness were a small guide to me as I, myself, achieved wealth. My brief breaking-and-entering career is only one of the coincidences in my life that I've kept track of. None for sure is as dramatic as this visit to Paul's house. I believe everyone has such serendipitous life events but some people just don't realize or keep track of them as they occur. For me, "the London job" was the highlight of my youth.

After London, Frank and I rendezvoused in Paris. We had made plans to meet at Napoleon's Tomb called Les Invalides on August 16. We would go there every hour on the hour until we found each other. And like a movie it happened. We spent the next few weeks of the summer touring Europe, visiting other parts of France, Italy and the Netherlands. It was a wonderful time in my life; a relief from the pain caused by my father's death.

Summer romance can be bittersweet. Fall semester I went back to NYU while Frank remained in France, as planned, for a study abroad semester. I thought of us as a long-term relationship, but he did not, and sent me a crushing, heartbreaking Dear John letter through the mail.

I went through so much during my freshman year. Love, drugs, activism, sex, study, travel, death and despair. Sophomore year was a letdown. What I remembered most were the books, not the boys. In the end, I was alone.

In my junior year, I transferred with a full scholarship to Brandeis University in Waltham, Mass. I wanted a change. Entering as a junior tended to make one an outsider. I didn't make any lifelong friendships there as I had with Mona and Lenni at NYU. However years later, I did connect with Cheryl Levin through the Brandeis Alumni Club, Lee Brooks through LinkedIn and Teva Benshlomo through Facebook. And when I was in medical school, I dated a Brandeis grad.

However, Brandeis did influence my choice of career. I had reached a crossroads. Math, after my sophomore year, became increasingly theoretical and I knew that it would not be my career path. I had left home thinking that I would use my math skills to become either a teacher or an actuary.

Nevertheless, not long after arriving at Brandeis, I became aware that every third student, both males and females seemed to be pre-med. "There must be something to this," I thought to myself. After further investigating the possibility, I decided to switch to pre-med. It was a late choice so I had to cram many science courses, such as organic chemistry and biology into my junior and senior years. That meant I had to wait until I finished my senior year to take the MCATs, the medical college aptitude tests, in order to score well. Then I would apply for admission for the fall class of 1974.

The year after graduation I worked doing research at the Commonwealth of Massachusetts State Laboratory Institute in Jamaica Plain, near Boston. My job as a laboratory technician was to assist in developing an improved tetanus immunization for the United States Armed Forces. To this day, I can't believe that I injected vaccine particles into mice.

Becoming a doctor obviously appealed to me. The chief reason was never to be poor again. I thought that this was an unusual, though an authentic motive to become a physician. I have learned throughout the years that many of my classmates and colleagues had the same driving force. Still, medicine was a logical choice because I always found science fascinating and I wanted a challenging career.

So, I applied to medical school. Getting in wasn't easy. Acceptance meant excellent grades, high scores on the MCATS and good recommendations. Brandeis issued composite recommendations, compiled from grades and test scores that were paired with professors' personal letters. I did not rate one of the university's coveted "superior" recommendations yet did manage to fall into the "strongly recommend" category. At least I surpassed the lukewarm "Why don't you become a biology teacher?" rating.

I got two medical school interviews. One was at Hahnemann School of Medicine in Philadelphia, which later became Drexel University School of Medicine. I tend to freeze in situations like this. Nevertheless, when it counted, I rose to the occasion. Dressing feminine, I thought at the time, would be a key to success during the interview process. It was just an intuition. But it turned out to be a good call.

I had come to New Jersey and was staying with my mother for the interview. It was a snow-covered morning. The drifts must have been two feet high. I called into Hahnemann to inquire if my interview had been canceled. "No." was the definitive reply. My mother was worried about me driving in such bad weather so my Uncle Hashel drove me there. I defied convention and wore a short knit black long-sleeve dress, with boots, pink tights and a blazer instead of a dark suit. I thought I looked great and would make an impression, assuming I had a male interviewer.

Dr. Demetrius Saris was enchanted with me from the first hello. What was supposed to be a 30 minute interview turned into a 90 minute dialogue. It was routine until I started asking him about himself. He told me about his career and family and how he had married a fellow physician, which was unusual in his day. I learned that everybody likes to talk about him or herself. I had a very good feeling about the encounter and my chances of admission. He recommended me to be accepted to Hahnemann. If I had not gotten into med school I would have probably gone into finance. It could have meant more money but would definitely not have offered the status of a physician. It is so odd how a stranger can have such an impact and significance in my life. I often thought of Dr. Saris but never bumped into him during my four years at Hahnemann although occasionally I would ask his son Steve, a fellow medical student, about his father. I saw his name once more. It was in the "In Memoriam" section of a recent edition of the Drexel alumni letter. I only met him once, but he changed my life forever.

So in 1974 I entered medical school. It doesn't seem so long ago but when I mention that women made up only 10 percent of the class, it does seem like a generation ago.

Meanwhile, medical school proved to be as tough as advertised. It required lots of memorization and hard work. Yet, I made certain not to neglect my social life, as I did not want to graduate without a "Mrs." degree to match my medical degree. This was not an easy task for me as men seemed to find me intimidating just because I was a medical student.

I hit the books hard in school, living in a studio apartment above a greasy spoon Chinese restaurant. I learned more from people than from books. I still recall the first mistake I witnessed. An elderly woman with excruciating pain showed up at the Hahnemann Hospital Emergency Room. She had not been to a doctor since giving birth six decades earlier. Diagnostic tests revealed that she was suffering from colon cancer. The resident physician decided to give her morphine, ordering 40 milligrams of the pain reliever, instead of 4 milligrams, a 10 times dosing error. The patient went into cardiac arrest and died. I will never forget the lesson of "the power of 10's." Not once in my career have I ever made that type of dosing error, perhaps the only positive thing to come out of that tragic event.

Another medical school memory was the first time I assisted in childbirth. Someone forgot to tell me that, days earlier, the baby had died in utero (in the womb.) Then I witnessed a blue mass being delivered. I was in shock until one of the doctors finally mentioned that the baby was already known to be dead.

Another assignment was to observe in a pediatric neurologist's office. I remember parent after parent coming in and complaining that their kids had learning difficulties in school. One vivid memory was of a mother relating that she had a deep, dark secret to confess. My mind immediately filled with visions of early trauma, child abuse, or strange ritualistic practices. Then the mother tearfully admitted that after being weaned from the bottle, her child had adamantly refused to drink anything but Coca-Cola for two years. She concluded that the soda dispenser in her basement had caused her son's academic problems. As a devoted Coke drinker myself, I ran from the office and doubled over in hysterics.

I also learned lessons in how to deal -- and how not to deal -- with people in crises of life and death. As a medical student in 1976, I naively answered a man's question about when his wife, suffering with cancer, was going to die. When asked, I naively predicted she would be gone in three or four days. The man responded that I was the only "doctor" with the guts to make a prediction like that. Just then, I realized I was in over my head. I told him I was only a medical student without a lot of experience. He didn't care. He praised my gumption since he was able to better prepare for her death. She happened to die after being ill for months on one of the days I had forecasted.

My best friend in medical school was Linda Alexander. We shared our struggles and triumphs. Linda was a health nut even back then, obsessed with nutrition and exercise. We have kept in touch over the years. She recently retired and opened a yoga studio. Linda is a breast cancer survivor. She knows firsthand that cancer is indiscriminate; it strikes and affects even those who eat right and stay fit. As I've always said, "age and health are life's great equalizers".

Another friend I've kept in contact with is Stanley Naides who went on to a prominent career as a clinician and immunology researcher. He was one of the few who enjoyed medical school for the academic challenge. Most of us only thought in terms of career.

Our joke was that we went to the "Big H" medical school, meaning Hahnemann not Harvard. Medical school in no way qualified as fun, yet it was more than worth the effort. It ultimately gave me a satisfying profession.

Meanwhile, like the other unmarried women in my class, I was on a quest to find the right man. Another friend of mine entrusted me with her secret involvement with an attending physician. Twice during rounds, I envisioned them in bed together and had to excuse myself before I keeled over with laughter.

During my third year, I went alone to a singles night at Doc Watson's Pub in downtown Philadelphia. (It closed in 2010.) There I met an optometry student named Bill Rapoport. We talked most of the evening and he impressed me with his concern for his family in Connecticut. The following weekend he thrilled me with a whirlwind date to New York City where we went to the Whitney Museum and Central Park.

Six months later, we were engaged. We married during October of my senior year. The following spring, my husband along with my family watched me graduate from medical school. I had gotten both of my wishes.

I realize now and to some extent then, how randomness truly played a major role in my life. If I hadn't met Frank at NYU, I would not have traveled to Europe in the summer of 1970 and had my whirlwind experience at Sir Paul McCartney's house. And if Frank hadn't rejected me, I might not have transferred to Brandeis, not have gone to medical school, not have met my husband, not have moved to Florida and not have won the lottery.

5. We Can Work It Out: Pediatrician, Wife, Mother

I didn't end up in Florida by accident. My third year of medical school was full of big decisions. One was to pick my specialty. I decided that year to become a pediatrician – you know, a doc who plays miniature golf on Wednesdays. I always liked working with children and it seemed like a natural fit. Meanwhile, my romance with Bill was blooming into a serious relationship.

When I mentioned that I must soon plan for my residency, he said, "Why don't you do your residency in Florida? I want to move back there."

Though he had been raised in Connecticut, Bill had already spent a few years in Miami, earning an undergraduate degree in business at the University of Miami. After working as an accountant, he decided to change course and pursue a degree in optometry at the Pennsylvania College of Optometry in Philadelphia. It wasn't surprising for him to "eye" this as a second career. Bill was born into a family of optometrists. It was the profession of his grandfather, father, Uncle Irving, his brother Steven and cousin Alan.

I knew he had good reason to seek the sunshine. As a child, Bill had been diagnosed with Wilson's disease, an inherited condition in which copper accumulates in various body tissues, chiefly the liver and the brain. A then-experimental drug, penicillamine, saved his life and turned the disease into a treatable chronic condition. However, Bill frequently developed pneumonia, especially in the winter, and said he felt much better in a warmer zone. Still, picking up and relocating to Florida would be a big step for me.

"What am I going to move to Florida as?" I asked him.

"What do you mean?" he equivocated.

"As a girlfriend?" I asked.

"Sure," he replied.

"I'm not going as a girlfriend," I stated emphatically.

Two days later he proposed. The truth? Most men need a little encouragement.

Jackson Memorial Hospital offered me a residency. So, in June 1978, we were on our way. In the back of my mind, I thought that someday we would return north, but we never did. I think about this every so often when Bill and I are having one of those typical, low-key marital disagreements, and I will say to him, "I'm the one who won the lottery, you know."

Bill will come back with, "Well if it wasn't for me, you wouldn't have been in Florida to win."

"Then I would have won the Pennsylvania lottery," I retort.

We settled in South Florida. The first years were a mindless blur. The residency consumed me. It was brutal. In those days, we would work 36 hours in the hospital, go home, and be due back the next morning. Every third night was an overnight shift. I hated when older doctors said that in their day, they worked every other night and how easy we had it in comparison. We sometimes worked 100 hour weeks. Today the limit is 80 hours. I try not to induce eye rolling in today's interns and residents by pointing out how much tougher things were in my day. No one wants to hear about the old days. It makes me realize how my life has come full circle.

I was intense, like Dr. Christina Yang, the character played by actor Sandra Oh in *Grey's Anatomy*. Except, I didn't have all that steamy hospital sex (I was married). I had no personal time at all.

Residency is basically modern day indentured servitude. The payoff was that I gained a lot of experience and saw many exceptional cases. One infant I treated was on death's door with severe dehydration. His mother had a vision of his impending demise and brought the infant to the Pedi-ER just in time. After his hospitalization, I followed the boy in my clinic for the next two years. During one of the visits, his 16 year old mother asked how old I was. I told her 27. She asked if I had children and I told her that I did not. She replied, "Dr. Press, I can't believe you are so old and don't have any children." This was a preview of things to come.

I made a conscious decision not to get pregnant during those three years. I wanted to be a top-notch pediatrician and I seized the opportunity to soak up as much knowledge and experience as I could from my residency. My intuition told me that motherhood would have divided my attention.

For the first year, we lived across from Jackson in Cedar Towers. The rent was $225 a month for a two bedroom apartment. It's still there but is now called Jackson Medical Towers.

Even though going through residency was hell, I bonded with my fellow sufferers, such as Drs. Ruth Schobel, Bill Llosa and Carlos Tellechea. We are all still friends and frequently reminisce about "the good old days."

My pediatric residency included attending weekly education conferences. Some lessons learned from veteran physicians stood me in good stead – but not always in the way one might imagine.

One lecture I remember was about how to thrive in private practice. The featured speaker was Dr. N., a well-known pediatrician in the community. I liked him from the moment my eyes looked his way. He must have been in his late 40s to early 50s and ran a very successful group practice. He had one of those craggy, handsome faces, blue eyes and graying brown hair. He wore a wrinkled brown corduroy blazer with khakis. I remember thinking he was sort of good-looking considering his "advanced age." He spoke with confidence. I found him at once both charming and arrogant. He kept looking my way and I had the feeling he liked me as well. When he invited us third year residents to visit his group practice, I felt as if it was a personal invitation.

A week later, I called his office to set up a five day rotation. I could have been matched with any of the group's doctors, but when I arrived, I had been paired each day (randomly or not) with him. As I shadowed him, I was impressed, maybe a little in awe. Dr. N. cranked out patient after patient in a most personable manner. He told me all about himself and his family. In addition, he showed an interest in me as well. Everything was going great -- until Timmy showed up.

Timmy, an 18 month old baby, was brought to the practice for a routine checkup. Dr. N. examined him and then told me to finish up the visit. One thing of note: some of Timmy's teeth were decayed. That was unusual in such a young child. The doctor assumed it was because of how he was being fed.

As Dr. N. made his exit, he yelled at the mother, "Stop giving Timmy a bottle at night."

The mother began to cry and said to me, "Dr. Press, I never give him a bottle at night. I take him to a pediatric dentist who is working on his teeth. I am very concerned there is something wrong with him."

I had noticed more than Timmy's dental problems during the exam. His hair was sparse, mere wisps. On reviewing his medical history with his mother, I gathered other pertinent information. He had been hospitalized three times for high fever with no apparent cause, even after the standard work-ups were done.

After studying his chart, I asked the mother, "Would you be interested in getting a second opinion from a pediatric geneticist?" I suspected something might be wrong but wasn't sure.

"I would be very interested. I would really appreciate it if you could set up an appointment for us," Timmy's mother replied.

I took her phone number and planned to make an appointment with Dr. Paul Benke, the pediatric geneticist, at the University of Miami. If there was something wrong with this baby, he was the doctor to see.

I then caught up with Dr. N. and told him of my plan for Timmy. His response, "Do what you want to do, but Shirley, you are wasting your time. I can tell you there is nothing wrong with that baby."

A few weeks later, I met Timmy and his mom at the university medical center and helped them navigate their way to Dr. Benke's office. He took one look at Timmy and exclaimed, "Oh my God, this baby has hypohidrotic ectodermal dysplasia."

I was astounded since I had never heard of this disorder but quickly learned about it from Dr. Benke. It is an inherited disease in which there is a lack of sweat glands. It results in frequent fever, and abnormal hair, teeth and nails. Dr. Benke performed a skin biopsy, which confirmed the diagnosis.

Although there is no specific treatment, there are guidelines to help those living with the disorder. Luckily, this condition does not affect intellect. However, because those with the disease are not able to efficiently cool themselves by sweating, care must be taken not to get overheated. The mother was relieved and assured that she hadn't been doing anything wrong.

"Now I know it isn't me," she said, thanking me profusely.

A couple of months later I bumped into Dr. N. at the hospital. After the initial greetings, I said, "Wasn't that interesting about Timmy?" hoping for a "well done," or a hearty "good job."

His response, "Sure."

Then he quickly said goodbye and never spoke to me again. Perhaps, he felt I was putting him down or pointing out his omission. Or maybe he felt that I outshined him.

Even at the time, I knew his ego was bruised by the turn of events. But I thought he was better than that. I remember thinking back then, "What will I do when this happens to me?" Another doctor makes a diagnosis that you've missed. Well, it has occasionally happened to me with the residents I teach. Every time it occurs, I'm reminded of Dr. N.

My method of handling the situation is that I compliment the resident on being an astute practitioner - praising him or her in the manner that they deserve. I surely know that is what I needed at the time of my training.

While the hospital was my life, Bill was building his own career as an optometrist. He worked with two ophthalmologists. However, that practice always seemed to be jinxed. One of the doctors died of cancer in his 50s. Not long after, the remaining physician failed to show up at work one day. He was an avid swimmer who routinely drove from his Miami Beach home to a nearby hotel pool, then went back home to change before making his way to the office. When he didn't arrive that one day, they knew something was wrong.

Bill called me. "Can you go look in the trauma center? See if there is anyone there matching his description," he said.

I sprinted to the trauma rooms, and there he was, critically injured, from being hit by a truck. He survived, but could never resume his practice. Bill went on to buy a solo practice in North Miami, where he worked until after I won the lottery.

One year in Cedar Towers was enough. We bought a house, on West 46th Street in Miami Beach for $71,000. We lived there from 1979 to 1986. When the residency finally ended in 1981, I was offered a good position in a nearby practice with Dr. Ann Eggert. During this time, I continued to work part-time at Jackson's Pedi-ER which was then called the Pediatric Walk-In Clinic.

I enjoyed working with Ann. However, the practice finances were a mess. Her good nature was the main problem. For some reason, we had many divorced parents on our patient roster. In those days, insurance didn't cover most of the bills, so patients paid up front. The mothers would say that the fathers would pay and vice versa. Too often no one paid. Our accounts receivables just grew and grew. Bill came to the rescue, a white knight armed with calculator and pencil. He volunteered to clean up the books and instituted a better billing system.

Private practice was rewarding. However, I chafed at being the second banana. Everybody came to see Ann. Eventually, I began to have a following of my own. Then I took hold of another opportunity. One day in 1982, Dr. Julia Rosekrans, the director of the Pedi-ER, tapped me on the shoulder. My first thought was "My boss! She's going to complain about something," and I could almost feel my self-esteem deflate. Instead, she recommended me for her job as she was leaving for an opening at the Mayo Clinic. I later learned that I was the second choice. The first doctor turned it down because of the money. I had to laugh at a another helping of being a second banana.

Nevertheless, it was a hard decision. I liked the rapport I had with "my" kids, especially watching them grow and develop. Their parents appreciated me and began to know me as a person, as well as a doctor. That usually doesn't happen in the ER -- although we do have our share of "frequent fliers."

Yet, I knew I would never again have that chance. Most directors had completed Pediatric Emergency Medicine fellowships and I did not, but the job was offered to me based on merit. I didn't consider doing a fellowship after I finished my residency because it meant another two to three years of training and I wanted to start working as a pediatrician. Being serious and intense finally paid off. It was all in the timing. I figured that if the director's job didn't work out, I could always swing right back into private practice. Looking back, the job gave me unique opportunities. Jackson is both the main teaching hospital for the University of Miami Medical School and is Miami Dade County's public hospital. It draws patients from every walk of life.

I was 31 and younger than all of the part-time attending physicians I supervised. I knew I would have to spend at least a year or two proving myself. And just when I finally got comfortable in the position, the hospital decided to contract out the ER operations to a private medical firm that offered full-time attending physician coverage. Though I half hoped they would lay me off, I stayed on as a liaison physician for the Pedi-ER and also became director of the Child Protection Team that deals with child abuse.

I became an expert on child abuse. Besides examining and making diagnoses of non-accidental injuries in children, I was also their advocate testifying in family and criminal court approximately 50 times in those two years.

On two cases, I had the opportunity to work with former US Attorney General Janet Reno when she was the state attorney for Miami Dade County. I was very impressed by her passion for the abuse victims. She also had one of those photographic memories for people. I've bumped into her a few times since my child abuse days and would say "It's nice to see you again. I don't think you would remember me but we worked together..." Each time she interrupted me and stated, "Of course, I remember you, Dr. Press. How are you?"

One case I remember well concerned an infant girl who was in a major car accident. The car was totaled and she banged her forehead on the dashboard although she had been placed in a car seat. She was rushed to another hospital. The radiologist there said her CT scan revealed a pocket of blood in her brain called a subdural hematoma. However, this doctor read the scan as an old injury, unrelated to the accident. The patient's neurologist then referred the case to the state with suspicions that the girl had been abused. After she was hospitalized, the state assumed custody of the girl and placed her in foster care. The case was brought to my attention because I was the child abuse consultant for the county. I interviewed the parents and was impressed by them. They also underwent scrutiny by the Child Protection Team. After reviewing the case, I decided that the CT scan needed to be read by a pediatric neuro-radiologist I knew of at another hospital and so I schlepped the films across town to meet with him. This doctor was a nutty professor type with a stellar reputation.

He told me, "Don't tell me the history of this case. I want to be unbiased."

A week later, this doctor called and stated that the scan was ambiguous and could be acute or chronic trauma. I then told him about the car accident. He said there was no doubt; the injury was the result of the accident.

The neurologist somehow developed a feeling against the mother, disapproving of some of her life choices, and insisted it was child abuse. He, in fact, called me and said, "Shirley, you are making a big mistake."

This really upset me as I had always admired this physician.

"I'm sorry," I said. "I'm going to go against your advice."

I reported to the state authorities that, in my opinion, the abnormalities on the CT scan were a result of the car accident and not abuse.

I thought that had ended it. However, adding insult to injury, when the parents went to pick up their child from the Department of Children and Families, the staff couldn't find her, at first bringing out a little boy -- a child not only of the wrong gender, but also of the wrong race.

The parents were soon in my office screaming and ranting, justifiably so, threatening to go to the newspapers and sue the hospital. I cut through the red tape, got their baby back, and that was that. It was like an episode of *ER*.

See Appendix "A" for more of my most challenging cases.

Before our kids came along, I began writing articles. It was an opportunity, so I took it. Over my career, I have had more than 25 academic papers and chapters published. The first case I wrote up was an unusual situation in which a hair from a girl's scalp fell out and wrapped itself around her clitoris so tightly she risked losing the tissue. We carefully incised out the hair and her condition was resolved.

One of the attending physicians, Dr. Phil Paul, and the pediatric dermatologist that we consulted, Dr. Larry Schachner, suggested I take a photo and write up the case. Easier said than done. Larry made me rewrite the case report five times. After the last revision, I finally said, "This is it. This is the best I can do," while vowing never to talk to "that slave driver" again. A few months later, he tapped me during grand rounds to say that the journal *Pediatrics* accepted our paper. Moreover, he gave me the first author position. Needless to say, we continued to work on papers and research projects together for many years afterwards.

Meanwhile, the time had come to start a family. It wasn't as easy as I had hoped. Now that our lives were stable, I couldn't get pregnant. After some treatments, I could get pregnant, but couldn't stay pregnant. Only those who have experienced this can understand the devastation. It seemed that everyone, including my sister and my best friend Marsha, was having a baby. In vitro fertilization was relatively new in those days and the success rate was not good. After a couple of years, we decided to adopt.

I contacted obstetricians in my area, put ads in newspapers, called adoption lawyers and then applied to a reputable adoption agency called Golden Cradle. We went through all the background screening, supplied the required documents and were accepted. They told us it would probably be a year's wait. To our surprise, they called us a few months later and told us a woman walked into the agency seven months pregnant and had decided to give up her newborn for adoption. She picked us from among many hopeful would-be parents.

Unexpectedly, I was pregnant again, but spotting. We decided to take the baby. One month later and a month premature, our son arrived. He was 5 pounds, 14 ounces, and the cutest thing you ever saw. He was pretty scrawny but it was love at first sight. He was everything we could imagine. There was only one problem. He was the slowest feeder ever. Johnny Carson would keep us company for an hour each weeknight while feeding Gershy his nighttime bottle. We named him Gershon in memory of my father. It is Hebrew for "a sojourner there." Gershon in the Bible was the eldest son of Levi who was the son of Jacob and brother of Joseph. This is not to be confused with the name Gershom who was the firstborn son of Moses.

We hired our first babysitter based on her experience with children. Mrs. Richardson was a Haitian woman who had raised eight children. I told her that her main job was feeding our son. No problem. By the time he was 8 months old he had grown into a chubby, happy baby. It was the only time in his life he was plump, as he was destined to be a slim person. Once he started cruising around, he thinned out again.

Meanwhile, that spotty pregnancy, to my delight, continued and seven months later Sarah was born. It was a rough pregnancy. Morning sickness became as much a part of my daily routine as putting on makeup. Sarah was three weeks early. I fell down a couple of steps at home two days before she arrived, and proceeded straight to the hospital. They said everything was fine and sent me home. However, a day later, I panicked when I didn't feel the baby move. I sped to the hospital, but by the time I arrived, she was moving again. Still, the doctors said they would induce labor the next day as tests showed Sarah was mature and almost full-term. As soon as they gave me the drugs to bring on labor, Sarah began having distress. That meant an emergency C-section. She weighed 5 pounds, 15 ounces. A few days later, my mother came to help out. I felt blessed, but overwhelmed. In one year, I had somehow gone from no kids to two wonderful little babies. It was really demanding.

Sarah was a small baby, though she was a good eater. Our new housekeeper, Lillian, would always remark at how smart she was. I taught her the alphabet when she was 3 years old. She always loved words. It used to make me laugh to watch peoples' reactions to what they evidently thought was a baby genius. Sarah, who at this age, could have been mistaken for a one year old, would startle people in the post office when she began reading letters off the posters.

I had fun dressing her like a little doll. I was always buying feminine and flowered outfits. I particularly remember the Polly Flinders smock dresses. I sometimes even bought matching mother-daughter dresses. But Sarah was never very enthusiastic about my choices and at 3 years of age stated categorically, "Mom, no more dresses. I want to wear pants." That was the end of that era.

She loved Gershy and he loved her. They were so close. They were in the same grade though different classrooms. They were in Little League together, took piano lessons together and played for hours on end. They were each other's best friend.

For vacations, we'd visit my mother in New Jersey and one summer the kids stayed with her and went to day camp with their first cousins, Andy and Maddie, my sister Barbara's two older children. Josh, her third child, was a baby at the time. They also got to know their second cousins, Jonathan and Jennifer. Otherwise, we would go to Orlando twice a year, every year. Like many of our friends, we were Disney connoisseurs.

Looking back, I can't believe how energetic and determined I was, both at home and at work. Despite having two young children, a husband to care for and a full-time job, I decided to tackle the Adult Emergency Medicine Boards. At that time, there wasn't a board examination for the subspecialty of pediatric emergency medicine. Pediatric Emergency Medicine boards did become available later on and I passed those in 1994.

Afterward, I wrote about my experience. Here's my original piece, title and all. It was written by hand in December, 1989.

Thoughts on being a Modified Superwoman and Passing the Emergency Medicine Boards

Since learning that I passed the oral exam portion of the Adult Emergency Medicine Boards and am now double boarded in general pediatrics and adult emergency medicine, colleagues have been coming up to me and asking, "How did you do it?"

I am tempted to say, "Oh, it was nothing."

But that just perpetuates the myth of the superwoman – one who has a career, husband, and children and even manages to pass these competitive boards with, seemingly, no sweat.

The tale began in 1987 when one of my colleagues asked me if I was going to take the Emergency Medicine Boards. It was the farthest thing from my mind since I was overloaded with a job, with the kids, Bill and the old house always needing repairs.

"I don't even know if I'm qualified to take them since my career has

been forever in pediatric emergency medicine," I replied.

He said that he had read the requirements, which allowed one to "grandfather" or "grandmother" into the board certification process under the practice (experience) clause and it looked like a go. After reading the notice of qualification, it did seem like my years of pediatric experience would count. To double check, I called the American Board of Emergency Medicine and they verified that I met the exam criteria.

They did give me a caveat that most of the exam was on adult medicine. Of course, I was excited at the prospect of being board certified in two specialties and being among the rare class of double boarded docs. Then reality hit. I would have to learn adult emergency medicine! It's not the same as pediatric medicine. Of course there is considerable overlap, especially in toxicology, environmental medicine and infectious diseases. But children are not miniature adults. They have different illnesses. For example, chest pain in an adult is usually associated with heart problems; in children it is more likely to be an infection.

So I decided to get some practical experience. The Emergency Care Center where I work is divided into four sections: Adult Medical, Surgical, Gynecology and Pediatrics.

I first set out to the Medical ER. I approached the attending physician and said I would like to see some patients.

"What is your background?" he asked.

"Pediatric ER," I replied.

He said, "That's good enough. Go see that patient over there."

After all, an extra hand is an extra hand.

Over "there" was an old geezer reeking from alcohol and complaining of abdominal pain. The first thing I learned is that I'd rather have a baby vomit on me than a drunk. But overall, it went pretty well and I learned a lot.

My experiences in the Surgical ER went even better. They really appreciated someone who could put an IV in any size patient.

I soon also realized that I would need to read a textbook on emergency medicine if I had any sort of chance of passing the written exam. After analyzing my schedule, you didn't need to have a BA in mathematics – as I have - to figure out that I had no time to study. Something had to give.

I went to my boss, Dr. Lee Worley, and asked for time off. He immediately looked at my flat stomach with a puzzled expression. The last time I made a similar request was when I was pregnant. I then explained how important it was to me to pass these boards. He agreed and was somewhat relieved. So in October, 1987, after two weeks of intense studying, I traveled to Atlanta, where the written part of the exam was administered, to give it my best shot.

As we arrived at my hotel room, the bellhop asked me if I was going to see the sights of the city. I told him I was there for the emergency medicine boards.

"How many times have you taken it?" he asked me.

"This is my first and only time," I replied, figuring it didn't hurt to have a positive attitude.

"I'm sure you will pass." he replied, as I gave him his tip.

The morning portion went okay. At lunch I was seated with four other physicians. The discussion entailed which preparatory courses each had taken. When asked, I said that I hadn't taken any.

"You didn't take a course?" the astonished docs chimed. My confidence plummeted.

After the afternoon session, I and several others took the van to the airport. It felt like we had all been to a funeral, especially since some docs had already taken the exam at least once before.

The weeks passed. Then, the day before Christmas, 1987, the notification came in the mail that I had passed. I could hardly believe it myself.

Now it was time to think about the second part of the exam, the oral part, which was scheduled for the following fall.

That September I went back to Dr. Worley and asked for more time off to study. I hadn't told him I passed the first part because that's the way he is. He doesn't ask you much. So he granted my wish a second time. This time I went to Chicago.

It was not my day. I was very nervous. It seemed like a combat zone. Examiner after examiner bombarded me with cases. It was worse than being up all night in the Pedi-ER seeing sick patients. I had no idea if I was on the right path when I gave them my answers. I guess I wasn't. Weeks later, I found out that I failed the test.

"I am still a good physician and a good person," I had to reassure myself.

The only thing I could do was try again the following year. The next September I went back yet again to Dr. Worley and told him I failed and asked for a few weeks of working part-time. He agreed but grumped, "What's it going to be next year?"

I was thinking, "How about jury duty?" But I didn't say anything.

This time I took a boot camp course which really helped prepare me. After several days of answering a barrage of questions, I felt more confident. I passed the second time around.

It's been a struggle. I'm exhausted and emotionally drained from the experience of studying three years in a row for these boards. I know it was all self-induced. I wanted to have these boards under my belt but didn't really have to do it. Knowing that I still can do it at age 38 feels great. My brain is not lettuce. I'm proud of myself and the modified superwoman that I am. Moreover, when a resident will occasionally ask me what are my hobbies -- there is only one answer: sleep.

The outsourcing of the Pedi-ER proved a failure. The only good thing to come of it is my friendship with Dr. Reina Lipkind, who was the director of the Pedi-ER for those two years while I did the child abuse work. Then in 1989, I went back to my old job.

Committees were part of the job. The ER and the Department of Pediatrics needed representation on various hospital and medical school committees.

Dr. Akram Tamer, one of the veteran attending physicians at Jackson, recommended me to take his place on the Quality Improvement Committee. I met him in 1978 when I was an intern and we have maintained a good rapport. We seemed to hit it off right away, and early on, we would discuss cases, academic papers and career choices. Later we'd talk about investments strategies and stock picks.

The QI committee focused on a variety of patient care issues. One was that Medicaid, the health care program for the poor, was rejecting a high number of Jackson's claims. This concerned the hospital administration as it meant Jackson was losing revenue. They needed someone to review the denied claims and "refudiate," as Sarah Palin would say, its decisions. The hospital was willing to pay $25 a chart.

I and another young doctor, Larry Friedman, took on the task. The charts, along with all medical records, were kept in the hospital's basement. Every day during lunchtime or after work, Larry and I would go down there and find charts piled up on a bookshelf awaiting our review.

The first time it took me an hour to write an appeal. But pretty soon, I knew what I was looking for and could do it in 15 minutes. For weeks, Larry and I would both go down to the basement. I did about 400 charts in 12 weeks. That's $10,000.

One day, I went to the basement and no charts were on the bookcase.

"Where are the charts?" I asked the secretary.

"Dr. Press, there are no more charts," she said. It was like a horror movie.

"No more charts – that's impossible," I continued. "You are still way behind. What happened?"

"You two got so expensive, we hired a nurse to do the job," she explained.

Of course, that made sense from the hospital's point of view. If we had continued, it would have cost upwards of $80,000 a year.

I called Larry.

"Larry," I said. "It's over."

"What?" his reaction being similar to mine.

As always, take the opportunity when it comes. It may not come again.

I ran into Dr. Tamer and thanked him for recommending me for the committee. He was caught by surprise.

"You actually like being on the committee?" he suspiciously inquired.

"Sure, learned a lot and the money came in handy," I replied.

"What money?" he asked dubiously.

I explained how writing appeals had become a lucrative sideline.

He was shocked. He stated that he used to do that for nothing. Oh well.

As the years went on, administrative duties and endless paperwork, its unruly offspring, took up more and more of my time and I had fewer workdays dedicated to practicing medicine. I eventually reserved one day a week to work a 12-hour shift treating patients. I liked caring for the stream of kids who came through our doors, which kept my clinical skills honed.

A day in the ER had a rhythm all its own. A team of doctors, nurses, residents, interns, technicians and secretaries manned the front lines. My typical clinical shift went something like this: starting at 8 a.m. and ending at 8 p.m., residents would present patient cases to me. I would re-examine the kids and we would discuss the diagnosis and then formulate a treatment plan. There was an unending cycle of children who came through our doors day and night. I was once asked how we advertised for patients. I was polite and answered that we don't need to. The person just didn't get it -- patients are always there, some days coming out of the woodwork.

The day's first patient might be a child with a cold. I would examine the youngster and reassure the parent. The second could be an infant with a high fever and we would diagnose an ear infection, "otitis media," in medical lingo. Then an asthmatic child with wheezing might appear. Then another otitis media. Then maybe a broken bone. Then *another* otitis media. Then another and another. If I saw 30 patients, every other one seemed to have fever and otitis media. At times we joked, that otitis media single handedly kept us in business.

There would be the typical childhood mishaps and illnesses: a kid fell off the bed and broke his arm; a child with high fever caused by pneumonia; a toddler with a viral infection. Patients suffered from sickle cell anemia, diabetes, seizures, and heart disease. Sometimes, we had to resuscitate a pediatric patient. We had our share of sudden infant death syndrome, child abuse, meningitis, seizures, drownings and overwhelming infection. Children in serious car accidents, with gunshot wounds or with other traumatic life-threatening injuries would go straight to Jackson's Ryder Trauma Center. Minor and moderate trauma came to the Pedi-ER. In addition, there were crossover cases like smoke inhalation and burns. It takes a while to know the system.

The ER doubled as a clinic for the adjoining neighborhoods so a good deal of our patients had routine childhood illnesses. Many of the non-routine medical cases were fascinating. I saw medical diseases that I would never have witnessed had I stayed in private practice.

Once, we had a 9 year old boy transferred from another hospital's emergency room because of a near-drowning episode. The patient was on a swim team and was pulled from the bottom of the pool by his coach. Fire rescue was called. After he was stabilized, it was noted in the emergency room that his heart rate was only 40 beats per minute (80 is normal) though he was awake and alert. Swimmers don't usually "drown." They know how to swim. If they do drown, it's typically due to a seizure or some other medical condition. In this case, we diagnosed the patient with a heart block and admitted him to the Pediatric Intensive Care Unit where a pacemaker was implanted. Then one sharp resident asked his parents about his droopy eyelids. "He's always had that condition," his mom responded. The doctor then consulted with the ophthalmology service for an explanation of the lid lag. His diagnosis turned out to be Kearns-Sayre Syndrome a very rare genetic disorder of muscle cells. It had affected the muscle in his heart and caused the heart block. It was the only such case I ever encountered. In his teens, the boy developed diabetes as a complication of this syndrome and tragically died a few years later. Experience and keen observations enabled the Nancy Drew in us to emerge.

Being the director of the Pedi-ER entailed a lot more than met the eye. I was psychiatrist, life coach, financial consultant, medical consultant, private physician to the staff, troubleshooter, confidante, bearer of ideas, soundboard, arbitrator and job matchmaker. I had an open door. People would plop themselves in my office and tell me all their problems. I am a great secret keeper and therefore can't divulge the many things that were told to me. It definitely added spice to my job.

Over the years, my respect for the Pedi-ER's nursing and support staff grew. They not only did their jobs. They did so much more. The nurses are on the front line at the triage desk. They are the ones who first recognize a really sick patient and alert the physicians. They also inform us when someone is going downhill or just doesn't seem right. They convince parents to let us do necessary procedures and do their share of translating Spanish and Creole. And who gets the credit? The doctors. Nearly all of the nurses and techs are also raising children and go home to the second shift of housework, homework, cooking and spending time with the kids. I suppose, like me, the side effect of "having it all" is chronic exhaustion.

One of my informal skills is job matchmaking. My former secretary, Eileen Gately, went to night school for years and finally earned a bachelor's degree from the University of Miami when she was in her mid-fifties. She applied for a management position on the Child Protection Team when I was the director there. The administrator wasn't sure she was the right fit. I talked him into giving her three months on probation. It worked out so well that she stayed on for many years.

A dreaded part of my job was scheduling. It took forever and no one was terribly happy because of the weekend and night shifts. I discovered that my friend Dr. Linda Robinson, who headed the medical emergency department, was earning extra pay for the time she devoted to scheduling. I went to my boss and asked if I could get additional earnings for my scheduling duties. No, he said; because I was technically a University of Miami employee, while my friend was a Jackson employee.

"So if a Jackson doctor does the scheduling, they could get the extra pay?" I asked.

"Yes," he said.

It took about a nanosecond for me to outsource this job. Realizing that one of my colleagues, Dr. Nirit Swerdloff, had a talent for this as she had demonstrated during her stint as chief resident, I hired her as the master scheduler. Nirit and I were both better off with this arrangement. It was a perfect match.

Occasionally my matchmaking skills failed. One doctor in particular comes to mind. I hired her because she seemed to have it all; stellar recommendations, a wonderful bedside manner and an interest in research. I thought she was a dream come true. She turned out to be a bona fide nightmare.

The first hint came during an informal gathering for doctors and their families. Midway through the party a bewildered colleague approached me and said Dr. "Smith" was hitting on her elderly father.

Not long after, a doctor moonlighting in the Pedi-ER reported that one morning, as he was resting in the on-call room, Smith opened the door and said, "Do you have your clothes on?"

"Yes, my scrubs," exclaimed the startled doctor.

"Too bad. I've always imagined you naked," Smith replied.

He later came to me. "I didn't know whether to rip her clothes off or send her out," he confided.

"I imagine you sent her out because you are telling me the story," I wryly remarked.

There were continued clues that pointed to emotional issues. Another doctor reported being stalked by Smith when they disagreed about a diagnosis. I was relieved when she left for another hospital.

But I wasn't altogether surprised when some years later the phone rang and Smith was asking if we had any openings. I said we didn't, though in fact we did, which Smith soon discovered.

"Why didn't you tell me the truth?" she later demanded.

At a loss for a moment, I had a sudden brainstorm. "The nurses don't like you," I said. She accepted that and found work someplace else.

One of my sayings in life is "always take lunch." I had approximately two lunch meetings per week. The other days I would eat with fellow doctors, nurses or friends from the hospital. The greasy spoon choices were: Jerry's Deli, a fast-food Chinese place or the hospital cafeteria.

I often ate with Jean Hannan, a nurse practitioner. Though we weren't that far apart in age, I became a kind of mother figure to her. She had lost her own mother when she was just a young child. Jean kept me in the loop of what was really happening in the Pedi-ER - stuff a boss is usually unaware of. "So what's going on?" I'd ask, after we had caught up on our personal news. Then she would give me the lowdown.

I saw other doctors who worked through lunch, like my mentor Dr. Nancy Fawcett, who I nevertheless admired for her clinical diagnostic powers. I needed the break. I needed the socializing. I was ahead of my time on this. For years, I realized how important these kinds of interactions are for mental health and foresaw what scientists are only now documenting.

I always encouraged our focused and sometimes overwrought residents to eat lunch outside the ER as well. "Don't worry, nothing will happen to your patients," was what I'd tell them, the inside joke translating as, "don't worry, probably nothing for your patients will get done -- until you come back to do it." Every job needs its touch of humor.

Even now, I try to eat lunch out with friends twice a week though I generally eat very little during the day if left to my own devices. After age forty, I realized I have to work at keeping thin. People are always asking me how I maintain my weight. My reply, "I don't eat much." They think I'm kidding but I'm not.

One of the roles I liked about my job as director was having a voice in making policy. However, the seemingly endless meetings took their toll. Sometimes, to keep my mind from wandering I would list common meeting phrases, like "think outside the box," "let's form a committee to look into that" and "we have to work as a team," and checked them off as they came up.

The meetings were what I least missed when, 10 months after I won the lottery, I gave up the directorship and became a part-time attending physician working in the same emergency department. Paradoxically, I've found in some ways that I have less time than before. It seems like I'm always doing chores. I sit and wonder how did all these tasks got done when I worked full-time. Well, I did complete a lot of them during work hours and didn't think anything of it. Then I read an article about businesses losing money due to pilfering by their employees. I was thinking how much do paper clips and pens really cost a company? However, the article was about stealing company time when employees do chores on the job. Light bulb! Consequently, stealing time must qualify me as a petty thief.

It began to dawn on me how much time workers pilfer. People who wouldn't think of stealing medical supplies however, read their personal email, day trade, arrange carpools, chat with friends and do their chores during the workday. Jackson even made it easy, having a bank, post office, medical bookstore and dry cleaner right on campus. Now that I'm doing these things on my own time, the chores seem to have ballooned. Hence my motto, "life is a series of chores" was coined.

The kids grew up and Bill and I worked. Our children then set off in different directions. Gershon attended a private high school that gave him more individual attention and Sarah entered The Scholars Academy, which is part of Miami Beach High School. Gershon attended Miami Dade Community College but college wasn't for him. Sarah, on the other hand, was accepted early decision to Cornell University and enjoyed her four years there. When she went to college, the lottery burden was lifted since her new peers were unaware of the event.

Until I won the Florida Lotto, I was like any other working mother, consumed with the day-to-day chores that must be done to earn a living and raise a family. I knew I was luckier than a lot of people. I had a career that, despite some frustrations, I usually loved.

Although my career was rewarding, monotony was creeping into my days in the ER. I had reached a plateau. There was nowhere for me to advance. Promotions were rare. My superiors were staying in their jobs forever. On the positive side, I had made friends with a core group of wonderful people, even though most of the friendships didn't extend beyond work.

I once told Dr. Valerie Thompson, a friend and colleague, "You probably won't be moving up to my job anytime soon unless I'm killed in a car accident." Who knew?

Sometimes I wonder how different my career might have been had I stayed in private practice. I think I missed out building long-term relationships with members of my community by not being a primary care physician. But did I make the right move? I think so. I wrote articles and chapters that were published in medical journals and books, of which I'm very proud. This wouldn't have happened if I stayed in private practice. Besides, I wouldn't have won the lottery either and I was so ready for the Lotto win when it came along.

But alas, it didn't mean our family was on easy street. We had financial security, but we also discovered we had a problem no amount of money has been able to solve. Gershon became addicted to drugs.

6. I'll Cry Instead: Gershon

Last night I gave Gersh $100 to basically have what he said would be his last binge. He was so threatening in the car when I picked him up from the hospital, where he had been taken to by the police. At that point, I gave up and gave him the money. It takes a lot of strength not to give money and know your kid will be on the street. I am so on edge. I cannot eat which is good.

That was my diary entry from Oct. 18, 2008. Gershon, my handsome, 24 year old son, had relapsed again after being off crack cocaine for seven months; dropping out of welding school at the same time. I had picked him up from the hospital after he had been involuntarily admitted because of his out-of-control behavior; banging on our door, screaming and cursing that he had nothing to eat. He was also in violation of a previous restraining order taken out against him by Bill. It was an especially heartbreaking moment because, seven months prior in March 2008, we had been able to celebrate Gershon being clean for a record-setting 14 months.

If winning the lottery, a lightning bolt of luck and timing, was one of the high points of my life, Gershon's drug addiction is its dark twin. Scientists believe there is a genetic predisposition to addiction, and I think that is true. Moreover, it is a disease that seems to strike vulnerable young people before they know they are at risk. That is what I believe happened to Gershon. Furthermore, there is randomness to it as well. If the drugs hadn't been available, would he have moved past those teenage years when most addicts get hooked? My life is plain awful and the irony is that I have all this money. I feel so alone and nobody can understand this drug problem unless he or she has experienced it. I wouldn't understand it myself.

Not a week goes by that I don't cry about his life and what his addiction has done to our family. It is so far from the hopes I had for him when he and Sarah together celebrated their Bar and Bat Mitzvah on Dec. 20, 1997 at Temple Beth Shalom on Miami Beach. This is the speech I gave that day.

Today as I stand with you two on the bima, I have so much love and pride in my heart. It seems like yesterday that we had been married for seven years and were quite dejected about not being able to have children. And then in the course of one extraordinary year the two of you came into our lives. And then we felt whole, or maybe a little more than whole. We felt so blessed. And as I stand here in front of you today, we still feel blessed. To watch you grow into the young adults that I see before me has been the best part of my life. And it seems like these 12 and 13 years have flown by.

Sarah, you are an amazing person. Not only are you intelligent and pretty, but you are truly a virtuous soul. When it came time to write down

13 mitzvahs that you have accomplished, you could have written a hundred. I am not surprised how well you learned your Torah and Haftorah portions, because you instinctively knew that becoming a Bat Mitzvah is the most significant thing in your life so far. That you not only learned it all months in advance also did not surprise me. And the fact that you are helping others and have expressed a desire to continue to help others learn their parts also didn't faze me. But what did pleasantly surprise me was that you willingly practiced with Gershon so that today could be a true collaborative effort for the two of you. Your love and devotion for your brother is exemplary. If Joseph in your Torah portion had been humble like you, the adversity that he suffered may have been prevented.

Gershon, you have given us a different perspective on life. You are also an amazing person. Not only are you artistic and handsome, like Joseph in your Torah portion, you are also a good soul. I was pleasantly surprised how seriously you took on the mission of learning your parts to become a Bar Mitzvah, even though most of this mature attitude came within the last few weeks. But the bottom line is that you're accomplishing it. You're learning that hard work pays off. The cooperative spirit that you've shown working with your sister makes me so proud of you. I hope that the two of you will always love each other as you do now. You have many gifts - your capacity for making friends, your sense of humor, and your artistic and musical talents. You should use them wisely.

I'm proud of both of you for the responsibility you took in becoming B'nai Mitzvah. But this is only a beginning and I'm glad that you told me that you intend to continue your Jewish education and plan on going to Israel as part of the Confirmation Class. Your trips to the Holocaust

Museum in Washington have given you a sense of what it means to be
Jewish and what my parents, your Bubbie and Zayda, and our aunt and
uncle, Tanti and Uncle Hashel experienced as victims and survivors of
the Holocaust.

I'm very proud of you today and I love you both very much. I know
you will grow up to be responsible members of the Jewish community.

I feel like the B'nai Mitzvah speech jinxed us. A few months later
Gershon started smoking pot just as he also began experiencing learning
difficulties. Frustration in school led to anger. We took him to a child
psychiatrist who diagnosed him with learning difficulties and a mood
disorder.

It didn't seem like 13 years had passed since the day we adopted him
at 9 days old. He was a dream child. He was even featured in a 1989
Miami Herald story about children's names. The reporter noticed him in
his nursery school class because he was so engaging. During his early
childhood and elementary school years, Gershon was happy,
participating in normal childhood activities like Little League and
skateboarding. He played the guitar and the piano. He was quite artistic
as well, often painting and drawing.

He learned to read early and was a superior speller. In fact, he was the
spelling champion of North Beach Elementary School. These talents
masked the academic problems that began to emerge in his early teens.

Whatever the cause of Gersh's school problems, we knew we had to
get him into a better environment. After seeing him struggle through
seventh grade, we enrolled him in the Allison Academy, a private school
with small classes. Yet difficulty with learning combined with his drug
use, which we didn't know about, proved a wildly destructive

combination.

Looking back, I realize that winning the Lotto when Gershon was a high school junior did not help him at all. My first instinct was to protect my kids from the publicity, which I thought would be the most harmful consequence. I explained to both of the kids that I thought their lives should go on as normal. Bill and I had discussed the situation and agreed that we didn't want to decrease their motivation to succeed by spoiling them.

But for Gershon the lottery win played into situations that were already dragging him down. He developed a sense of entitlement deciding that my win was *his* win. He wanted to spend money frivolously always asking for more and more. We were like his own personal ATM. I'm sure other lottery winners have had the same problem. We tried to steer Gershon on to a healthier path. In February of 2002 after problems at home and school mounted, we enrolled him in a wilderness program in Idaho for kids with behavioral difficulties. Participants were forced to learn survival skills, sleep in tents in the dead of winter and learn to take care of themselves. Gershon did well there. In fact, he may have saved another student's life. One morning he found his friend cold and blue and started banging on the door of the director's office. The boy was immediately rushed to a hospital and was treated for hypothermia. After Gershon returned home, things seemed to go well for a while. He did all right in school and made new friends. He may not have been academically gifted, but he was definitely not boring.

Then an odd and unsettling coincidence occurred in August 2003, just after Gershon graduated from high school. We were on vacation in Atlantic City. Gershon met a girl on the boardwalk. She turned out to be Brandi Bragg, the granddaughter of Jack Whittaker, who had won a $314 million Powerball jackpot in 2002. She and a friend invited Gershon and his friend to join them for a ride in one of the trademark rolling chairs that are pushed up and down the boardwalk. They are an Atlantic City tradition. The four of them spent some time together and would have probably seen each other the next day except that we were leaving. As instructed, Gersh told no one that his mother had won the Florida Lotto – not even Brandi who had her own lottery story. Tragically, Brandi died of a drug overdose the next year. This is one of many weird happenings or coincidences in my life. In Appendix "B", I describe others.

That September, Gershon began using crack cocaine and almost immediately became addicted. A friend of his gave him some crack to smoke and that was it. We suspected that he was using marijuana but had no idea about the crack. He enrolled in community college, but it was clear from the get-go that he wasn't cut out for it. He tried a few trades. Some, he found too demanding. Others he just didn't like.

We found out he was on cocaine in May 2004. The police brought him to a nearby hospital and he was involuntarily admitted under Florida's Baker Act, which can be used to force someone into psychiatric care if they are deemed likely to harm themselves or others. Gershon was cutting his arms with a knife in the lobby of his girlfriend's apartment building. His drug screen revealed cocaine use. I was and wasn't shocked because that was the probable explanation of his erratic behavior. I naively thought that with treatment he would overcome the crack use. Moreover, he was already scheduled to attend the Benchmark Young Adult School in Loma Linda, Calif., which offers academic and lifestyle assistance to young adults.

From May 2004 to Sept. 2005, he stayed at Benchmark, which also helped with developing skills for maintaining sobriety and the nuts and bolts of thriving on one's own.

From there he moved to Virginia with his friend Mike and got a job as a stocker in a local supermarket. He returned to Florida and worked as a painter's apprentice until August of 2006 when he relapsed again.

In October, he was arrested for possession of crack. On December 5, 2006, Gershon was in a halfway house after spending five and a half weeks in jail. For him this was relative freedom before entering a rehab facility. Gershon has self-destructive tendencies and at the last minute, he gives up on things. I feared that he would never get to the van that was supposed to take him to the rehab facility. I awoke early that morning to pick him up and drive him to the spot where the van would be waiting. The van stop was ten minutes away from the halfway house. Gershon, surprisingly, was ready. We were carrying his bags to the car when he told me that he had to make yet another trip back to the room to pick up his radio. I said, "No, just leave it." for fear that he would bolt. My heart sank. I feared that this procrastination signaled he had no intention of going to rehab. I panicked. I told his roommate, a guy in his thirties, that Gershon was self-defeating again. I was afraid of what was going to happen next. Gershon had purposely left his radio in his room. He finished placing his stuff in the car and was about to return to his room when his roommate greeted him with the radio. Having no other choice, Gershon got into the car and we sped away. With tears in my eyes, I mouthed, "Thank you." The guy had been in Gershon's shoes and truly was trying to help my son avoid his own path. This was the gift of the roommate.

Since high school, Gersh's life has been a roller coaster of jail, inpatient and outpatient treatments and entry-level jobs. In April 2008, Gershon was sentenced to a year of probation after a frightening incident.

April 4, 2008

He was violent during his last spree with crack cocaine; to get the police to respond to our reports of him stalking us and breaking into our home, we were required to get a restraining order. When he did return to the house, we called the police. It took four men, two dogs and a helicopter to find him only a few blocks from the house. Why can't he put all this resourcefulness to good use? He spent eleven days in jail, which also served as detox.

When I confided to close friends about Gershon's drug addiction, they were very surprised. They, like me, had a stereotypic image of what a drug addict is like. A while back, Gershon and I were having lunch and we bumped into one my friends. I introduced him to my son and then sent Gersh to order the food. Will said to me that he was amazed by Gersh. All he knew about Gershon was that he was my self-destructive, drug addicted son who was ruining our lives. It was hard for Will to associate that person with this one, so good-looking and charming.

Remarkably, Will and Gershon hit it off, talking sports, music, jobs and friends. Will even told Gersh that he would definitely call him to go to a sports game. As a caveat, I told Gersh not to count on it because I didn't want him to be disappointed. Will did what he said he would do. In fact, Will has become an older brother type of friend to Gershon. The two of them jibe in a way that Bill and Gershon do not.

Our friends Lori and Arnie Mishcon, an optometrist, couldn't say enough about Gershon's appeal when he went in for an eye exam. Lori, a former teacher, who works in the office, and Arnie both really liked him saying that he was the most courteous young man they had seen in a long time.

Gershon isn't the only polite drug user out there. A few years ago, Gershon's Toyota was stolen in Miami. He put the word out that we were offering a $300 reward for its return. It worked. One night Gershon called me at 4 a.m. to say someone had come forward. An hour later I was in the well-lit Walmart parking lot near our home, handing over cash to a nicely groomed young man -- of course another addict -- who graciously said, "What a shame it is to meet you under these circumstances." Even in drug addiction, there are occasional amusements. But it has been hell, not only for him, but also for all of us. Each relapse is new misery.

We found out most of Gershon's drug use history when he was in a recovery program that insisted on family counseling as part of therapy. It is very common for families not to know what was going on and then the shock hits. I can't believe this happened to us. My diary entries chronicle our family's long journey.

April 15, 2008

I am going crazy with my son. I look back at just the last several years and cry and cry over my son.

After Gershon got out of jail, he began working part-time. Then that June he signed up to learn welding at a trade school. After that, there were six months of remission before another relapse.

This time in December 2008, we sent him to the Drug Abuse Foundation in Delray Beach, Fla. for detox and rehab. After his release, he started a sales job and moved to his first apartment located in Davie, Fla. However, three months later, he was back on drugs.

The entire spring of 2009 was a struggle to get Gershon some kind of help. After several tries, I was able to get him admitted to an in-house treatment facility under the Marchman Act, a Florida statute that allows a judge to order a person into treatment if the court finds they are a danger to themselves or others, or that drug use has impaired their judgment.

May 22, 2009

I feel that I have lost my son. He has been in relapse for at least four weeks. This time is different. He is refusing help. Rehab is hard and he's gone through it a number of times. This time he wants to die. I tell him that he is breaking my heart, but he just responds that his heart has also been broken so many times. This past week we went to our daughter's graduation from Columbia's Mailman School of Public Health, where she received her master's degree. Meanwhile, I didn't know if my son was dead or alive. He was so far away from us. I missed him at the graduation, but not the way someone would miss someone who wasn't able to attend because they have cancer or some other medical disease. This felt different. Gershon just isn't part of our lives. It gives me great pain to admit this. The graduation came and went and he just wasn't there with us. I do want him back but I don't know if that will ever happen.

Today I attended a rehab center's relatives support group. I don't think Gersh is serious about rehab. It takes a lot of work and I don't think he's willing. Therefore, I'm going to look for a therapeutic halfway house setting. Just when everything was going right for him school, work, his first apartment, Bill back in his life, and Will in his life, he then self-destructs and goes back on crack.

May 30, 2009

This past Wednesday I was convinced Gershon was dead. Even in his most dire circumstances, he always called. If he lost his phone, he'd call collect. I checked his phone records on the Internet. No calls for four days. I called his friends. No one had heard from him. Nothing, no word, nothing. I called the police, but the reply was that this was not a missing person's case since there was no evidence of foul play. Someone's 24 year old son who didn't call his mother in four days just doesn't get much action. So I decided to look for him myself. Sarah mentioned that he was staying in South Beach. Then I spoke to a private investigator about finding him however, he was out of town. Therefore, in desperation, Bill and I roamed around South Beach in search of him.

We miraculously found his car. The PI said that he would show up at the car. However, it had three tickets on it for the previous three days. With no sign of Gershon, I first drove his car to my house and later that day decided to go to the Dade County's morgue. My friend Joan Bender came with me. I convinced the women at the desk that there was a real possibility. They had two unidentified males there. Just as they were leading me into the morgue, guess who called? Yes, my son. I was overjoyed to hear his voice. The women at the morgue must have thought I overreacted, but whatever. So now, my crazed, drug-addicted son was alive again. He suspected that we took his car, which was the only reason he called. Only this brought him back to me. These past days have been hellish trying to get him into detox and/or rehab. He just wants money for the crack. It has overrun his life and mine. I do not know if I'll ever get him back. I traded the nightmare of his death for the nightmare of his living. This drug has taken over his life and I'm afraid he is lost.

On July 15, 2009 after an initial assessment and evaluation, the court remanded Gershon to the country's rehab facility for 56 days. As far as treatments go, this program was rather long. Moreover, I came to a new understanding of my son during those weeks.

Aug. 20, 2009

I visit him twice a week. It is required by the state to have educational sessions prior to each visit. Although I'm annoyed by this requirement, I have to admit that I have learned a lot. Also I get to visit and talk to Gershon for a full 45 minutes each time and feel I am closer to him than ever. I learned all about his drug use, which started at age 13 with marijuana just months after his Bar Mitzvah. I feel that I cursed myself with that wonderful B'nai Mitzvah speech I had given about him and Sarah. His history reminds me of the movie "Reefer Madness" which mocked the idea that marijuana can lead to drugs that are more dangerous. Well in my son's case, it did.

I thought he started with drugs after high school but, in fact, he was smoking weed all through. The crack did begin however, three months after graduation. And it's been a dreadful ordeal since. I asked my son if I could write about him and he said absolutely that I should.

Then he said he wanted to read "Tweak" by Nic Sheff and talked about writing his own book. (Nic is the son of David Sheff, who wrote *Beautiful Boy* a book about Nic's drug use. Nic himself chronicled his addiction to methamphetamine in *Tweak*.) *Gersh would have a lot to tell. He has been through hell with this drug addiction. Homeless, beaten up by other addicts and by the police, starving and other adventures he wants to elaborate about. I said I thought it was a terrific idea and to get started immediately.*

I bought the book "Tweak" for Gershon and decided to read it myself before giving it to him. Here is Nic Sheff a bright, talented guy lost in the drug world. What he describes is a lot of what Gershon has been through. I was drained after finishing the book. I realized that our family has been through a similar hell to what Nic describes. Who in his right mind would want this for himself? Gersh does have potential but it has been wasted by crack. This brings me to the recently adopted premise that drug addiction must be a disease. There is no other explanation. The self-destructiveness, the anger, hurting everyone in your life, losing everything over and over again, the stealing, the dead friends, the addicted girlfriend, getting beat up, the detoxes, the relapses, the rehabs, spending holidays in rehab over and over again and the total hopelessness are all themes in the book and in Gershon's and our lives too.

In the end, it was Nic's parents who were instrumental in getting him help over and over again until the last rehab worked. They didn't give up. I feel this is one of my missions in life: to get Gershon clean. I honestly believe that he wants it. However, he doesn't even know what triggers him to go back. The tiniest thing can do it. Nic also writes about this phenomenon of relapsing when you least expect it. It is a devastating disease. For the past nine years, I have been absorbed into this drug world with him.

It's as if I am Gershon, my son. I put so much of myself into him but it just doesn't pay off. He is not a bad person. Gersh is hip to trends and is a cool guy. I love him dearly even though he is so unlike me. For example, he does not ascribe to the notion of delayed gratification. He needs a car. I suggested a Toyota as being appropriate for his stage of life. No, he wants a BMW. He doesn't care how old the car is. He just wants his dream "Beamer." Maybe he's right. What's there to wait for? Live for today.

I feel that he will always be dependent on me. And I, in turn, will always be there for him. Gersh got out of rehab on Sept. 9, 2009. Three weeks and two days later, he started to use again. He managed to take buses down to Overtown, a dangerous, drug infested Miami neighborhood, and again hung out at the crack houses. He called me on a Sunday morning broke, dirty and hungry, begging me to pick him up. He said that was his last time. How many times have I heard this?

The old adage is that addicts never really begin recovering until they hit rock bottom. I keep hoping that Gersh has reached that stage, but then another binge happens and the spiral starts anew. He loses or sells his possessions, becomes homeless, doesn't eat, doesn't maintain himself and becomes belligerent and depressed.

When he is on drugs and has no money he teams up with other drug addicts and shoplifts. This is new. This is why I don't hear from him for days, as this is how he gets money. Who knows what else he has done? When he is clean, he can't believe he has done this. He has also stolen money and jewelry from us. This is very typical and reflective of his addiction. It's hard to understand how a drug can turn you into someone diametrically opposed to who you are.

I am angry with my son for relapsing into drugs and being so self-destructive. Yet, I also feel sorry for him and for myself and I'm depressed about it. The meaning of Gershon's name applies. He is a stranger in exile. Sometimes I feel that being given up for adoption at birth has something to do with his self-sabotaging.

Things did not improve for Gershon as 2009 neared its end. In November, he overdosed on Thorazine, an antipsychotic medicine that a friend had given him and was beaten up. Again, I was able to get him into treatment using the Marchman Act.

But he constantly relapses. In early 2010, Gershon worked as a table runner at a restaurant that just opened. He didn't have a car at that time so when the buses weren't running late at night when he finished up with work, I was acting as his chauffeur. I keep going like the Energizer Bunny because I want to believe that one of these days it will work. He relapses even when things are going well – even when he has a lot of support from his doctor, Drs. Jason Radick and Fred Jonas, his sponsor, his lawyer Danny Jonas, his family and friends.

I keep lists and I see that Gershon has lived in 14 different places in the last seven years and has had six cars. He had accidents with five of them. When I analyze the course of events set in motion by the dismal trajectory of Gershon's life, the devastating toll it has had on our family becomes apparent.

My cousin Janet Coleman Kirschner and I decided there are four curses in life that begin with the letter "A": attention deficit disorder, alcoholism, Alzheimer's and addiction. People are lucky if they can escape these afflictions.

His drug use has affected me on many levels – depression, social isolation and my ongoing suffering in seeing him like this. A number of people that I have confided in about his problem have suggested I see a therapist myself. They are right, I should. The one positive thing Gershon's drug addiction has done for me is evoke compassion and understanding towards other addicts.

Some things barely catch the media's eye. One of them is drug addiction, which is a very grave problem in this country. We are losing a portion of our children to this disease. Where is the outrage? Where is the in-depth media coverage? I don't think anyone can truly understand this disease without personal experience. That's why most of the drug counselors are former addicts themselves.

March 21, 2010

It is March 21, 2010 and again I don't know if Gersh is alive or dead. We had a blowout last night. He was kicked out of yet another halfway house for another relapse. He stayed at our house for one night and went out and used again. He spoke to his sponsor but then didn't heed his advice. So after we picked him up from work, we confronted him. He promised not to use again. Then, when I insisted on no locked doors in his room and not going out, he got upset.

He demanded the money I took out of our joint checking account that I kept for him when he relapsed. I gave him a choice of the money and getting out or staying in our home without the money. Suddenly he started going through my desk looking for the cash. He was getting violent, punched his fists into the air. The drug has taken over him. Neither love, nor incentives like getting another car in a few months, nor reasoning, nor pleas, nor compassion, nor his sponsor or friends will move him. All he cares about is his next high. I gave him his money and he left. He let Bill drive him a mile away and he was off. Now, I am worried sick about whether he overdosed or if he is dead or where he is. He's not answering his phone or texts. It seems like I can help others but can't help my own son. I'm worried sick. I'm wondering how I can go on like this.

For the next year and a half it was much of the same – relapsing, not working and living in a halfway house near us. Then in August, 2011 Bill's cousins Jimmy and Debbie Keese offered to have Gershon move up to Daytona Beach and work for them in their business. It was bumpy but so much better for all of us. He relapsed there also but recovered. They did not give up on him. Total toll – 17 relapses in 9 years. I'm tired and disheartened and so is Gershon. He is ruining my life or some would say, I'm letting him ruin my life and he is definitely ruining his. In October 2012, he moved back to our neighborhood into another halfway house. At present, he is clean and looking for work. The cycle goes on. The feeling of impending doom never leaves me.

7. Can't Buy Me Love

Everybody fantasizes about what it would be like to win the lottery. Shopping for cars, houses, boats. Trips to Las Vegas, France, Hong Kong. No more 9 to 5. Doing whatever you want to do whenever you want to do it.

But did I foresee all the loonies and scammers who would leap out of the woodwork? Did I anticipate the schemers and sociopaths who would just pop into my life? No, not even this sensible Lotto gal saw them coming. I was eager to get more involved with non-profits but did I have any idea of what it would be like to step into the local charity circuit or should I say charity circus? No, I didn't see that either. We were expecting invitation after invitation. Instead, we received solicitation after solicitation.

Years after the win, I still can't believe it happened. I have mixed emotions about our good fortune. I feel good about it as well as guilty. Sometimes, I think that I will wake up one morning and it will all be gone. And then back to the old life.

Bill had closed his practice two years after the win and was spending much of his time looking after our finances. I'd stepped down from the Pedi-ER directorship ten months post-lottery, though I continue to work about once a week as a staff physician.

Friends sometimes ask why I keep working. I explain that it's my calling in life as well as my identity. I feel that I can't give it up right now. When you retire, you are no longer a practicing doctor. I've seen the most amazing physicians retire and they are basically put out to pasture. It is tempting to think that it won't happen to me but it probably will. The other reason is that my career is what I'm most proud of in my life, second to my children.

There are many opportunities that have arisen from working at Jackson Memorial Hospital. Like with many things in life, you have to recognize the possibility when it presents itself. Recently, the politics at the hospital gave me a chance to relive my student activism days. Jackson recently found itself in financial difficulties. The administration proposed to outsource the emergency room doctors and hire a for-profit group that submitted a low bid offer to supply ER physicians. A few of us "activists," met and wrote a statement opposing this plan. We also drummed up support for our cause of retaining our in-house physicians. I was pleased when Dr. David Woolsey, a colleague, asked for my input. I was present when our group made its case to the hospital's board. We were successful and they dropped that idea.

I have trouble letting things go. I usually allow something to go on longer than it should. While my job in the Pedi-ER is gratifying and the people I've worked with are great, I've been there and done that. It's been my second home, key to my identity and I have a great deal of trepidation over a final farewell. Unintentionally, I have become a subject of debate at work. I would say it's 50-50. Fifty percent say I should never work at all. The other 50 percent say they would do exactly what I'm doing - working part-time.

One of my basic premises is I always try to help people. Okay, I know this is hardly original. However, my good fortune snowballed into good luck for two other physicians at Jackson. When I stepped down as director of the Pedi-ER, Dr. Thompson became the new doc in charge.

"Good news, you weren't killed in a car accident," she joked.

Another physician, Dr. Hector Chavez, a previous part-timer, also benefited. He told me, "Your winning the lottery got me a full-time job at Jackson." It's nice when the dominoes fall in place.

Besides continuing to work, I resolved to learn more about charities and philanthropy. After we had given gifts to our families (like college tuitions to our close relatives) and friends and funded some worthwhile causes we finally devised a game plan. We decided to sample some of Miami's burgeoning cultural scene. We had long been interested in the arts community. But we had been too busy with work and the kids to do more than attend occasional concerts or museum exhibits.

Now, we could get more involved. We naively thought we might find kindred souls, cool intellectual conversations and new friends. Maybe a local art museum was not the place to start – or maybe it was. Bill and I are more French Impressionist than performance art. Still, a few years ago we decided to join a local museum after hearing an inspiring speech given by its director. We decided to attend its gala one December evening. It featured an exhibit by a lauded artist who worked in neon lighting. That sounded, well, electric!

The event was timed to coincide with Art Basel, the annual art event where high end galleries from around the world set up shop at the Miami

Beach Convention Center. It's a four day extravaganza that includes concurrent shows at local galleries, event spaces and museums. All sorts of people descend on the city including collectors, critics, philanthropists, high rollers and just regular folks.

"Let's go to this," I said to Bill when the invitation came. It sounded exciting. I was curious to meet "artsy" people. What's more, I could dress to impress with my vintage Gunne Sax dress and Frye boots. For those unfamiliar with Gunne Sax, this company made the most beautiful, romantic, Bohemian hippie dresses of the late 60s and early 70s. Most have gorgeous cotton print material and a full skirt. The best ones have lace and a corset top.

I bought several Gunne Sax dresses in vintage clothing shops and on eBay. Then there's the one I scrimped and saved for when I was in medical school in 1974, which I value the most. At that time, I weighed 100 pounds and wore a size 7. Now I'm 115 pounds and can barely squeeze into it. Therefore, today I buy size 9 dresses of the original Gunne Sax line. That would be my size today if women's dress sizes stayed consistent. However, as most women know, that didn't happen. I weigh 15 pounds more today and I'm a size 4 to 6 in the racks at Bloomingdale's or Macy's. That's two sizes below where I should logically be. This means that if you wore a size 14 in 1975 you're wearing a size 10 today (and a size 2 if you're shopping at Chico's). The manufacturers keep dropping their sizes. They call this vanity sizing. Do they really think they can fool the public? Well, I guess they have.

I chose my black Gunne Sax dress for the event. So off we went - Bill, the dress and I – to what I thought would be a small group of art enthusiasts in eveningwear. Instead, the place was crammed like the Times Square subway station at rush hour with, maybe, 3,000 people.

My dress and I were lost amidst the sea of capes, shawls, great clunky jewelry, real and costume, six foot tall women, men in kilts and people who seemed deeply impressed – with themselves – before they'd even seen the art.

And the art? I'm sure it was profound, but huge words in neon left me less than supercharged. Moreover, I felt like Tom Hank's character in the movie *Big* somehow out of my element.

"I just don't get it," I said to Bill. Did all these people actually like this stuff? Though most were talking to each other rather than looking at the art.

"It's like the *Emperor's New Clothes*," Bill said.

No matter, I thought, so we weren't "turned on" by the art. We could still socialize with other patrons. Interactions went something like this: I'd ask the person peering over my left shoulder what they thought of a piece. There would be a murmur or two and then they'd scoot across the room to greet someone they knew or just drift off. That's how most of the evening went. I thought we might connect with people when it was time to dine. Instead, it was a mob scene, or should I say snob scene, on the dark patio. In addition, absolutely nobody noticed that I was the 60s reincarnate.

Suddenly I thought about whether I really needed the attention. I love wearing my vintage dresses for myself so shouldn't that be enough? I guess not. I wanted someone to notice the dress and me, for the "chutzpah" it took to wear it. Then we could have reminisced about The Beatles, college, the "boho" look or some other random nostalgic topics of the 60s. We left disappointed.

In just a few years following the win, I've concluded that charities are confusing. There are so many of them. Actually, there are more than one million non-profit organizations in the United States. This includes schools and other institutions not considered official charities. Some days, it seems that every single one of them has our phone number.

I donate to approximately forty organizations a year and I'm on the board of three: the Florida Friends of the Israel Defense Force (IDF), the Jackson Memorial Hospital Foundation and the Miami Lighthouse for the Blind. The common advice is to become actively involved in a select few. But, I'm still a rookie philanthropist learning the ropes. For example, I've discovered that most board memberships require a sizable donation.

My friend Pam, who heads an education charity, has complained that she will spend time and money hosting people for lunch or dinner; they will commit to make a donation, but never follow through. That seems wrong.

Sometimes, I go out of my comfort zone and venture out alone. In one of these random occasions, I met Bonnie Clearwater, the director and chief curator of the Museum of Contemporary Art (MOCA) in North Miami. I had gone to a lecture which I thought was on women's rights. As it turned out, I got my wires crossed and the event, hosted by Bonnie, was on promoting art among underprivileged teens. My friend Dr. Shulamit Katzman (a pediatrician, mother of three, former model and fluent in eight languages) happened to be there and asked me if I wanted to join her and some friends for dinner afterwards where I was seated next to Bonnie. I found her to be charismatic and funny. We had an engrossing conversation about New York and the 60s. My friend Shulamit likely clued her in about the lottery win.

To my surprise, Bonnie sent me an email the next day. "So nice to meet you..." she wrote. A few weeks later, we met at the mall for sushi and decided to see the movie *Infamous* also known as "the other Truman Capote movie." We had a nice time.

It would have been fun to get to know her better but I realized that as a museum director, she always has major demands on her time. Nevertheless, it's good to see her at museum events. With Bonnie, I got a glimpse of her glamorous lifestyle. Yet, I'm sure her career has its own challenges.

I've learned to say no to relentless wooing if I'm not interested in the specific charity. Recruiters are always friendly when you are their target. It's so fake.

Nothing makes me feel more awkward than to attend women's luncheons alone, no matter how good the cause. It takes guts to go solo to these events. I go to learn about or support the charity, but I'm also hoping to meet new and interesting people even if it means sitting through boring award presentations. Sometimes, I want to leave early but I don't. After all, one woman sneaking out could lead to another tiptoeing away and before you know it, the whole South Florida charity luncheon system would collapse. I stay and try to strike up conversations with mundane questions.

"What do you do?" I asked one woman at a charity luncheon. She had no profession. "How many kids do you have?" I asked, figuring she was a stay-at-home mom.

"I don't have any."

"What do you do?" I replied, frankly intrigued.

"Play tennis, go shopping." Nothing in my experience, growing up or even now, can relate to that.

My criteria for these events are not high. If I have one conversation of interest, then it is successful to me. I am introverted, which has hurt me my whole life. I long to be bold and fearless, but too often I just can't do it.

It takes a bit of time to digest the charity lingo. Once, a group wanted to give me an award for "Best Doctor Ever" or something like that. I declined because the "honor" was really for winning the Florida Lotto with the expectation of contributions.

Ridiculous things can also happen at these charity events. Here's a classic. These affairs often include silent auctions. This is where people place their bids on a slip of paper next to an item. The goods are usually donated. When the auction time is up, the person who wrote down the highest amount wins the item. Sounds simple, doesn't it? At this particular event, I bid on a Ghirardelli chocolate gift basket and an orchid plant. I bid $35 for the orchid after two bids of $25 and $30. The increments on this plant were $10, so the second bid was placed incorrectly. My friend Reina and I were talking to some people and standing next to the orchid plant when the bidding ended. As they took away the bid slip, I could see that the winning bid was mine.

One hour later, I had my fill of the party and wanted to leave. I had also won the gift basket so I offered to pay for the items and take them home. The women in charge emphatically said, "No" and I'd have to wait until they made the official announcements. I insisted that I had to leave. So she said she would call to make arrangements for me to pick up the prizes, which were right in front of me. The next day someone called and said I could pick up the basket at their office, which is near the hospital. I mentioned I would also be picking up the orchid. The woman informed me that I had not won the orchid. I told her succinctly that I had won because I saw the winning slip with my name on it. A few days later at the pick-up, there was no orchid plant so I complained. She said she spoke to the director who explained that I made an illegal bid. I said the second bid was the illegal bid, not mine. Abruptly, I gave in after having had enough of this nonsense – so I just paid for the gift basket and left because I had to go back to work.

I couldn't help but wonder how they hoped to keep donors with such an attitude. I later repeated this story to a friend who suggested that someone at the office thought the orchid went too cheap and took it for herself not realizing that I had been an eyewitness to the last bid. It turns out that my friend was right.

A few days later, I got a call from the charity saying that my orchid mistakenly was given to the wrong person and I could call her to retrieve it. So I did but it turned out to be a wrong number. That was it. The orchid was not "beshert" or meant for me. It probably would have died quickly with my unorthodox gardening skills. This, my friends, is silent auction fraud. I should send this story to Hollywood producer Larry David as a subject for his series *Curb your Enthusiasm*, one of my all time favorite TV shows.

Coincidentally, this same charity looked to its volunteers and donors to review grant applications from local social service agencies. I had already done that one year and enjoyed it. The next year it decided reviewers would be required to undergo eight hours of training. I asked to be excused from this as I already knew how to perform reviews and was myself an experienced grant writer. They wouldn't give me a pass on the training. Needless to say, I finally gave up on that charity. It does, however, provide mileage as a conversation piece.

The charity that provides me the most satisfaction is a small foundation I started under the auspices of the Greater Miami Jewish Federation. My foundation, named for my parents, The Leah and

Gershon Press Holocaust Fund helps Holocaust survivors with health care needs not covered by insurance, Medicare or Medicaid. I have mixed thoughts on starting my own charity. There are already so many good ones out there. Do we really need another one on the landscape? Even Warren Buffet gave the Bill and Melinda Gates' Foundation a big chunk of money instead of duplicating the cost of running another massive foundation.

After a few years, the money somehow wasn't being utilized and was accumulating some interest. I called up and spoke to a director. "I want the funds to be spent," I told him, exasperated. "I don't want the interest. When the money is spent, I'll replenish it."

That made me realize how you have to stay on top of the charities to make sure your money is being used as you intended.

One of the most irritating experiences is when your money is remembered, but you are not. One big cheese in a certain organization calls me to donate again and again yet never recalls who I am when we're face to face. I bumped into this big shot at an IDF dinner and said, "Hi, how are you?" There was a blank. I said, "You don't remember me, do you?" He admitted he did not. I then reminded him of something unique we have in common. Only then did he recall who I was. He subsequently stated that I was "a project of his." Come on, if you're running an organization and can't remember someone you've talked to and met multiple times, what am I to think about the efficiency of this charity let alone the intelligence of the person?

When you talk to non-profit directors, development personnel or managers, you're left wondering if the rapport established is real or not. The answer often reveals itself when you don't hear from them until they ask for another donation.

Then there are the mail solicitations. Many are from legitimate charities - there must be someone in these organizations whose entire job is tracking down lottery winners. We received ingenious appeals, handwritten letters, pleas, and pitches both heart rendering and hilarious. You don't know which are real, exaggerated or totally out of left field.

We did agree to give a substantial amount to the Jackson Foundation. If you do give anywhere, it means you are letting yourself in for an endless, forever after wooing. Not a month after giving to some group, I usually get a letter asking for more money. I'm beginning to entertain the thought that some charities think the word "annual" means monthly. It makes you wonder if they blew your entire donation on stamps and stationery or on trinkets sent through the mail like little necklaces, greeting cards, magnets and return address labels. The worst is when they get the address wrong on the labels. It's infuriating! At least spend my (and other donors') money giving me something I can use.

At any rate, with charities at least you know your money is doing some good. That can't be said about the con artists who somehow found us. A little about myself: I stick to my promises. I help people as much as I can. Yet the "S" on my forehead must stand for "sucker or sap" rather than for Shirley.

We've been ripped off a few times. Besides giving people gifts of money, I've loaned people money that I'm not going to get back. That's okay. I then have to consider it an "unplanned gift." And you don't have to be a lottery winner, or even wealthy, to be taken advantage of.

The worst case that I am aware of came after I decided to buy a used car for Gershon from a mechanic highly recommended by a friend. "John Doe," who sold used cars from his garage, was friendly and even helped me with minor repairs. He said he could buy Gershon a car from an auction. He asked for $2,500 up front and then $12,500 after he found a car. In total, I gave him $15,000. That covered the cost of the car and his fee. I wasn't worried. My friend and her husband bought several cars over the years from this guy. But weeks, then a month went by and no car, no refund, though my friends reassured me the car would come through. When weeks turned into months, my friends were shocked. They intervened but with no results. Then John signed a promissory note with scheduled payments, but none arrived. So I filed a police report. The police said it was not a criminal matter but a civil case. Therefore, I wound up taking John to court.

Finally, the court date came and the judge ruled in our favor. No surprise there. John admitted in court that he owed me the money. John continued to stall and stall. The irony was that he now owed thousands more in legal fees, for both my lawyer and his own. I've received a total of $3,000. If you deduct my legal fees, I've recovered $200. Why did I take him to court knowing it would cost me legal fees and there was no guarantee of recouping the money? Because I don't like being ripped off. No one does.

The funny thing is John used to call me to "touch base" and promised the money was on the way. This must be the trademark of a truly talented con man. He even asked about my family and me.

Not too long ago I was in the kitchen when my brother-in-law Michael who was visiting and watching the news on TV exclaimed, "Hey, that sounds like Shirley's guy." Sure enough, there was John on the evening news arrested for allegedly ripping off a string of people. The police called the next day and asked me to come down to the police station and make another statement, which I did. "After you, he started ripping off others," said the officer taking my statement. It was rumored that he allegedly lost up to a half a million dollars gambling. I've learned - never pay upfront. The aftermath was that the other ten victims and I had our day in court in November, 2011. John was sentenced to 30 months in prison after he pleaded no contest to grand theft charges. The money? Probably gone forever.

People present all kinds of proposals to me. "I have a sure fire way for you to make a lot of money," the pitch always begins. What they don't realize is I don't have to make money. I'm happy with the money I have. There is an entire cast of characters with foolproof schemes who somehow found me.

One that sticks out in my memory is the man with the coloring books. This was after I won the lottery but before I stepped down as director. I was in my office at work and the phone rang. A man asked if I was Dr. Press. I said, "Yes." Then he proceeded to tell me that he had coloring books to donate to the Pedi-ER.

"When we take donations, it has to be a large quantity," I said. Otherwise, we've learned it generally isn't worth the hassle.

"How many would you like?" he asked.

"About 2,000," I replied.

"No problem," he added confidently.

He described the coloring books and they sounded appropriate so I said it was OK. He said he'd come to my office with the books. Well, a few days later a skinny guy in his 40s or 50s shows up, suspiciously looking like an old TV snake oil salesman. Moreover, he was empty handed.

"Are the coloring books outside the office?" I asked.

"Forget about the coloring books. I wanted to introduce myself to you because I'm the next Walt Disney!" he exclaimed, and then, before I could stop him, he went on and on about his animation company that just needed venture capital.

"You tricked me," I said.

"I had to get my foot in the door somehow because I know you have money," he said.

"I'm sorry," I said. "I don't deal with people like you."

"I'll bring the coloring books, I promise."

"I don't want the coloring books. I want you to leave."

"I have the coloring books."

I finally told him he would have to go through administration to make a donation. I called the administrator, Jeff Katz, and told him what happened just in case the coloring book "entrepreneur" had other schemes up his sleeves. He never called.

More traditional investment opportunities came our way, as well. One medical colleague, who I liked a lot, had decided to start a hospitalist company. Hospitalist is a fairly new medical specialty. It does fill a niche. A hospitalist functions as an in-house primary care doctor for hospitalized patients and is usually an internist, general practitioner or pediatrician.

"It sounds like a good idea but I have to see a business plan," I said. She was asking for $200,000 to get the company off the ground. She came back with a plan and I gave it to my financial advisor. He in turn ran it by his firm's banking experts. It came back with a big, fat, red "No" stamped on it. It was a good plan but the major insurance companies were doing the same thing and would likely do it better. So I passed on that one.

But there were missteps. One attorney acquaintance suggested we invest with him by providing a second mortgage to one of his clients who could not qualify for a bank loan. That should have been our clue. We would get nine percent interest on our investment after our lawyer would take his cut. He said that if his client defaulted, we would get the house. The client did run into a rough patch, however we didn't get the house and it took years to get our investment back. The anxiety wasn't worth it.

People are always expressing their opinions about being lottery winners. My cousin, Dr. Jeff Simonoff, husband of my first cousin Bev – the one we used to lose on the Atlantic City boardwalk when we were kids - is a professor of statistics at NYU. He has always said that buying lottery tickets is a waste of money. Unless… of course, you are that 1 in 20 million, like I was.

We've been very cautious and may have missed opportunities. I cringed when I heard about Bernie Madoff and wondered how supposedly sophisticated investors could risk their entire nest egg with one person. I would not put more than 20 percent in any one investment. Even though it's a lot of work, you have to diversify your investments and keep on top of them. Bill spends many hours a day looking after our portfolio and talks daily to our financial advisor.

The oddest thing is that I have bad credit. That is because my identity has been stolen not once, but twice. The first time was shortly after my win. We received a call from our credit card company to inform us that someone in the Midwest impersonated me with a duplicate credit card and bought a $1,000 money order from Western Union. I was able to trace it back to a gas station where my credit card had been out of my sight for a few minutes.

I ended up with bad credit but was able to repair it after going through the identity theft protocols. Recently it happened again. Someone with my stolen social security number was able to open an account and take out $300. I didn't even know I had the credit of a deadbeat until a New Jersey bank refused to let my mother add me to one of her accounts. I guess they felt I wasn't a good risk. So for the second time, I went through all the work to clear this up.

8. Day Tripper: I'm a Gambling Jersey Girl

Moishe, a poor, but good and pious man, prayed to the Lord every day, imploring, "Please God, let me win the lottery so I can care for my family and give to charity." Year after year, Moishe repeated the same plea and nothing. Finally, after much time had passed, a voice came thundering down from above: "Moishe, help me out. Buy a ticket!"

It goes without saying that you gotta play if you want to win. And who do you think religiously plays the lottery? It is gamblers and I am one of them. That is why we buy the tickets in the first place.

People are always shocked when a lottery winner loses their millions in a few years. I'm not. The phenomenon does not surprise me at all. Of course, not everyone who buys a lottery ticket is a confirmed gambler. But I would bet that almost every gambler plays the lottery. I have since 1988. The set of lottery winners and the set of gamblers overlap a lot more than most people realize. One of my determinations in life is not to be one of those self-destructing winners or whiners.

Perhaps more than others, this Lotto gal prides herself on being somewhat of a lottery maven. According to Malcolm Gladwell in his book, *The Tipping Point*, a maven is someone who reads up on a subject and knows more about it than most. I look for books and articles that discuss lottery winners. This research plus personal experience have taught me where lottery winners get into trouble. It's hiding in plain sight: gambling.

The wagering does not stop at playing the lottery. It's casino table games, roulette tables, slot machines, and betting on sports or horses. More crucially, it can be bad investments, stocks, real estate, new business ventures, and "lending" money to people and so on. We can gamble on anything.

A few years after winning the lottery, Sarah was watching *The Fabulous Life of Jennifer Lopez* on TV and asked me, "Why don't we live like that?"

"We're not rock stars, movie stars or sports figures where the money rolls in year after year," I reminded her. "Ours is a one shot deal."

Overspending is tempting. Luckily, it's not in my nature.

Bill and I were more prepared for the windfall than many people are. We were in midlife when the Lotto win happened and had long ago begun investing for our children's college education and our retirement, so we knew a bit about money management.

The irony is that the Lotto has allowed me to release my inner gambler that had been sublimated by the hours I spent working and raising a family. And it didn't take too much coaxing for the gambling Jersey girl to emerge.

I knew I enjoyed playing poker, blackjack and the slots from my very first trips to Atlantic City when I was 27 years old. You either like gambling or you don't. I had a feeling I would and I was right on target with that assumption. My next gambling experience was about a year later, when Bill took me to Las Vegas. But it wasn't to visit Caesar's Palace. Bill and his dad were attending an optometry convention. While the doctors Rapoport went to seminars and Bill's mom, June, went shopping, I hit the casinos.

The funny thing is that Bill doesn't like to gamble and doesn't like me to gamble. But he never thinks that, if I didn't gamble, he might *still* be practicing optometry and not have been able to retire.

Before I won the lottery, my only regular casino visits were to Atlantic City, where I would go with my mother and Aunt Ruchel. The daily buses ran from towns in New Jersey and Pennsylvania. It was a virtually free ride because the bus company gave riders $10 in quarters to play the slot machines and a lunch comp, which equaled the price of the bus ticket. We would make a day of it.

Day trippers really made up the bulk of the Atlantic City gambling clientele. Donald Trump reportedly wanted to court high end gamblers when he opened his upscale Taj Mahal casino in 1990, so he didn't include facilities for the buses. Then he realized that a huge percentage of revenue was from bus folks, especially retirees. So that policy soon changed. Almost every casino actually has its own terminal for buses. The Taj Mahal website calls them motor coaches.

Gamblers like to brag about their wins. It's half the fun. But sometimes it's prudent not to boast. That's what happened on one Atlantic City trip with Aunt Ruchel. It was a good day for both of us. I was at the blackjack table when my aunt came running over to find me.

"Shirley, Shirley, you have to leave the table and help me," she said. "I won 400 'silver' dollars and I can't lift them into the buckets." This was when the one-armed bandits still used coins instead of the vouchers they use today.

My aunt suffered from arthritis and had someone minding her machine for her. Luckily, it was an honest person. We naturally tipped her to say thank you. I had to leave my lucky streak at the table and help Tanti cash in her winnings. When we finished, it was late and time to head back to the bus.

When we got back to her house, my Uncle Hashel said, "So how much did you big gamblers lose today?"

"We both won," I responded.

"You two never win," he insisted.

And this Jersey gal left it at that.

Gambling is now my not-so-secret other life. I don't hide it from anyone. Though I don't talk about it that much either, except with other gamblers. I don't consider myself to be a diehard gambler, but I can put some folks to shame. Slots and blackjack - I could play those games every single day, 365 days a year, and 24 hours per day. Furthermore I'm not at all ashamed of it. But that is not how everyone reacts to my favorite pastime.

After all, I'm a well respected physician in town, a doctor to make my mother proud. I am a pediatrician, so children are obviously my first love. But, even a doctor has her vices. Gambling is mine. I figure I must have inherited this trait. I've tracked it from my great Uncle Jake to my Aunt Ruchel and then to me.

It's others who have a problem with my gambling. People who are casual friends as well as some of the people I work with were absolutely *shocked, shocked, shocked* that I gamble. But it doesn't hurt anyone and I'm not gambling with the rent money or the kids' college fund. Did I get rewarded, as so few people do, for a vice? Maybe.

I gambled very little before I had the means and the venue. It's hard to spend too much time at a casino if there is not one nearby. That's how it was for me during all the years before I won the lottery. Now it's a new situation. A few years ago, the Mardi Gras Racetrack and Gaming Center added slot machines. Not long after, Gulfstream Park, the Hallandale Beach horse racing track, opened a casino. Both are within a few miles of my home. So now, I routinely go several times a week.

The designers are clever. The casino does everything to appeal to the senses. It pulls you in from the moment you enter. It's full of neon lights that turn the surrounding darkness bright and sparkly. Without windows, the atmosphere is timeless. At Gulfstream there is an enormous round fish tank with lion fish and other exotic fish swimming about, adding to the feeling of weightlessness and timelessness.

Gambling is usually a solitary pastime. When I'm playing slots or video poker, I only concentrate on the machine's screen. I think of nothing else. When I get a phone call I get terribly annoyed. I don't care who it is. No question, it's an escape. I love watching the reels spin with its array of combinations. The machines have different themes. Some examples are Aztec Temple, Ancient Egypt, DaVinci Diamonds and Russian Treasure, which I like because it plays the Beatles' *Back in the USSR* in the background. Some machines are programmed to give you a lot of tiny wins called a high hit frequency and others to give fewer but larger payouts. It really doesn't matter. Your $20 is gone in a flash either way. Needless to say, when I win, it is so much fun.

Yet I do impose limits. I never take more than $200. When that is gone, so am I. I don't let myself use the casino's ATM machine. I put imaginary blinders on when I pass them. Moreover, I never play online.

Video poker is the game that calls me back again and again. I justify this craze by believing it is skill and not just luck that is needed to win at these games. There are many different versions of video poker and you do need to know which strategy is best.

Even on regular slots I feel you need an approach. Figuring out how many lines to play and how many coins to play must be considered in your line of attack. But the casinos do take advantage. A penny slot machine rarely costs you just a penny. There can be 20 lines to play so that's 20 cents and then you can play a multiple of this up to 20 times. So one spin on a penny slot can wind up costing up to $4.00. However, more lines usually translate into more winnings.

I go with my friend Joni who also likes to gamble. We eat together, chat a little and then go our separate ways -- off to the tables or slots. Sharing meals or snacks and talking about how it's going are the benefits of having a friend with you. But you don't need someone to gamble with you. You don't even *want* someone with you at the machines. It's not the kind of social activity that two people can share. If you do go with a friend, you want it to be someone who has the same focus on the games and tables as do you. Otherwise they can be a distraction to real gamblers.

I once took my old friend Jackie with me, because she had mentioned during a lunch that she loved slot machines.

"I'll just leave you here," I said, parking her at an interesting machine, eager to get to "my" machines.

"Wait!" she said. "What game do you suggest I play?"

It was clear she didn't know much about slot machines.

"What about video poker?" I said. "That's an easy one."

She opted for regular slots. It was like going with my mother. I watched as Jackie won $280 and didn't realize it. Believe me, a gambler she is not. I think I brought her luck.

I do perhaps bring others luck at the casino. It seems like a disproportionate number of players sitting at machines next to me win.

A trip to the casino with another friend, Cosma, was helpful in another way. She had somehow twisted her knee a few days before. It was so painful we took the elevator rather than walking up the steps. I had to guide her on her gambling excursion as it was her first trip to a casino. The odd thing was, by the time we finished, the pain in her knee had disappeared. A trip to the casino was better than an injection.

I usually go in the daytime. My fellow gamblers are mostly geriatric and retired. It's a walker and wheelchair city. The young people come at night.

I have become friendly with a few people I routinely see at the casinos. One elderly man at Gulfstream always singles me out for a friendly greeting.

"Having any luck today?" he asks.

"Not really. The machines are cold," I reply.

Conversations are always about the machines, if any paid out, and other related topics. Yet there is an instant familiarity with co-gamblers – especially when they win. Not long ago I was next to a woman who won $125.

"Do you believe this?" she said to me. "It's my birthday!"

"Cash it out, cash it out," I urged her, but I doubt she did.

Gamblers are encouraged when they are playing near someone who wins. It means at least some of the machines are paying out. And somehow you feel their luck will drift your way like fairy dust.

It's a different world. Yet sometimes my worlds overlap. More than once I've bumped into someone who is freaked out when they see me, either because they are so surprised to see *Dr. Press* at a casino, or because *they* are unmasked as a fellow gambler. I once saw the husband of an acquaintance who I knew had a regular job with regular hours.

"What are you doing here?" he said to me, a bit goggle-eyed.

"Oh, I'm here all the time," I cheerfully replied.

"Good to see you," he said dashing off.

The best day I ever had I won $5,000. I was down to my last $6 and won on one spin of five "7s." It was a progressive slot. My worst streak was losing 20 out of 22 hands at a four card poker table.

Is it an escape? Without question. But it's fun and I like it. So who is to judge? When I'm playing the slots, I forget about all my troubles. Gamblers are fools and I am one of them.

I do get mad at myself when I stay too long and lose money. So why don't I just leave when I'm ahead? Isn't that the commonality of all vices and addictions? If I lose, I get a let-down feeling, thinking about the time I could have used to catch up on my paperwork or work on my book. It robs me of time and money. But when I win, I feel vindicated.

Some people I know are problem gamblers. For those people and those who just want to stop, there's always the self-exclusion route. Most casinos now have an option for you to sign an agreement that will banish you from the casino for a year or a lifetime. It's the lap band for gamblers. According to the agreement's terms, if one manages to sneak past the guards and gamble, you can't collect on winnings. I occasionally think about signing on, but it's for people who can't control themselves and not for me.

I do think about the money I lose and how it could be better spent. But I don't care. Spoken like a true gambler.

You do have to report to the IRS winnings of $1,200 and over that occur on one spin. The casino at the time of the win gives you the tax forms. You can deduct your winnings from your losses. Good luck, bad luck or whatever. At the end of each year, the casino will also give you a statement of the total of your wins and losses. "Don't look at it until you get home," the woman from Mardi Gras warned me as she handed me my statement at the end of last year. She didn't know I can afford the losses.

9. Baby, You're a Rich Man

The message read "Julie Haire, TLC" with a phone number. Hmm, I thought, perhaps a pediatric facility named Tender Loving Care. After all, the note came through the hospital, where I was working a steady, but not busy, shift that April evening.

I looked again at the paper. TLC... could it possibly stand for "The Learning Channel" that produces the lottery show that I myself have watched? My heart skipped a beat just as it had done on Sept. 6, 2001. Could they be calling me? "No, never me," I thought, "Of course, not. They would never pick me."

I called the number. "Hi, this is Dr. Press returning your call," I said.

"This is Julie Haire, producer of *Lottery Changed My Life*," she said and proceeded to pitch the show that profiles lottery winners.

I didn't need much convincing. "I can't believe it, I can't believe it," I was inwardly exclaiming while Julie went on to say that her job was finding lottery winners she felt had a good story.

"Why do you think I'm a good story?" I asked.

"Because you are the only physician we know who's had a big lottery win. Are you interested?"

Yes, yes and yes! I was thrilled. The opportunity had come at the perfect time, just as I thought I was finishing my book. I asked her if I could promote the book on the show and she said yes, noting that people promote stuff all the time.

However, there were a few hurdles. Before moving forward Julie interviewed me for more than an hour over two days, asking all about the Lotto circumstances and our life afterwards. I was nervous and wanted to make a good impression. It was crazy!

Bill and the kids were a tougher sell, but I got them on board with the time-honored mix of bribes and persuasion. "No," was Bill's initial response. But I admit it; I poured on the guilt and called in all my marital IOUs.

"If you love me, you'll do it," I said. Poor Bill never had a chance and caved after about an hour.

It was all coming together. I was getting an opportunity for a second 15 minutes of fame and I was ready. The kids had moved out, I was working just one day a week and life had become routine. When I started the book, it dawned on me that part of being published would mean seeking more attention. By then, almost nine years after the win, I felt ready for whatever limelight could come my way. "Take the opportunity," the little voice inside me said.

Yet, I had shied away from publicity after winning the Lotto. It's the last thing you initially want. Bill and I had our hands full securing the money and making the necessary financial decisions. Though 9/11 news understandably dominated everything, I was still mentioned in various newspaper, radio and TV stories. One of my friends and colleagues, Dr. Carlos Tellechea, told me that he almost had a car accident when he heard my name announced on the radio.

I turned down all further publicity including *People* magazine mostly out of concern for the safety and the emotional well-being of Sarah and Gershon. And there things remained until the spring of 2010.

Events moved fast after I agreed to do *Lottery Changed My Life*. A date in early June was set, and I had just a few weeks to try and shed five pounds, figure out what to wear, and worry about what I would be like in front of the camera. A friend recommended I find a media coach. Mark, a buddy of Bill's, suggested Alyn Darnay, who runs a South Florida film production company.

I had a bit of trepidation. Alyn, a good-looking guy of my generation, turned out to be wonderfully practical. He gave me great tips like pausing and thinking before answering questions. I was also surprised to learn from my friend Renee Rotta, a former newscaster, that I twirl my hair when I get engrossed in a discussion. Good observations.

TLC sent a three man crew for a three day shoot. The first day they interviewed Bill, Sarah and me separately. Gershon had decided against being on the show. Sarah and I then baked cupcakes for the cameras. Conor, the producer, who conducted the interviews, kept asking how much we paid for various home furnishings. They must have been disappointed. Our house is nice, but there are no jeweled chandeliers, priceless Persian rugs or Picassos hanging around.

Later we went to the nearby Gulfstream Park racecourse and lunched at The Cheese Course, a casual, local restaurant specializing in cheeses from around the world. Sarah and I enjoyed a sampler platter. I would have had wine but Alyn had stressed not to drink on camera. So it was cheese and water.

The second day was all about my work in the Pedi-ER at Jackson

Memorial Hospital. Earlier they'd asked me to choose a colleague to interview. So I picked Rick Sobel, a nurse I'd worked with for 20 years. I called him on his cell.

"Rick, this is Shirley from work. If someone asks you about me, do you think you could say something nice about me?" I asked.

"Why?" he deadpanned.

I told him about the show and that the producers had asked me to scout out people to talk about working with me.

"Of course I'll do it," he said.

During the hospital taping, I examined a patient. Then they filmed me exclaiming over and over and over, "I'm Dr. Shirley Press and I won 56 million dollars!" I felt ridiculous but that's show business.

The producers had me re-enact the scary death threat phone call I received at work. Shereese and Mirda, two of the Pediatric ER's nurses and Bonita, one of our secretaries, all helped out to re-enact scenes around the lottery win.

That evening included dinner at Joe's Stone Crab on Miami Beach with friends Carol and Ira Price. Joe's treated us like royalty. Eddie Witte, the maître d', was exceptional. The TLC crew urged us to order a bottle of wine.

"You have to be celebrating," Conor said. I gave in, despite Alyn's advice.

I later told him and he clarified that wine was okay. "Just don't have drinks," is what he had said.

The final day was back at the house where we re-enacted my car brakes being tampered with. We walked around the neighborhood and later they interviewed me in my home office where I spoke about the book. The whole experience was exhilarating and fun but nerve wracking and exhausting. I never realized how much work it takes to create a short segment of TV.

I got more and more nervous as the show's airdate approached. Alas, it was on the same night as the Emmy Awards. But what can you do? I'd made dinner plans with a friend, Karen C. Bill was out of town and afterward my friend Renee and her boyfriend Neil had us over to her apartment to watch the show and celebrate with tiramisu and champagne.

Time crawled. Finally, *Lottery Changed My Life* came on. But where am I? I thought. We viewed the upcoming clips and I didn't see myself. "Oh no," I said, "They've scrapped the piece."

My worst fears. The ultimate humiliation. I can live without being on the show, but I informed almost everyone I knew that I was going to be on. Finally, just before the next commercial, there was a quick promo with a glimpse of Shereese and Bonita of the Pedi-ER staff. At least it's going to air. Of course, then I worried about how I was going to be perceived.

Suddenly, there I was. "Yay," we all yelled, jumping up and clapping. It is totally awesome to see yourself on national TV. I wasn't too bad and Sarah was terrific.

The editor spun my story a little. I, like the other participants, went from poor to wealthy – if you start with my childhood. But since I am a physician they saw it as going from rich to richer. I was a bit disappointed that the part where I talked about the book came in the show's wrap-up but that's OK.

"You did great," my friends assured me as I finally relaxed enough to sip the champagne and dig into the tiramisu.

I was glad it was over. The response was fantastic. So many people called or emailed me. My childhood friend Deena called and said, "Can you imagine a poor girl from Camden on TV?" I too could hardly imagine it myself.

Timing is everything. Reporter Wendy Grossman from *People* magazine called in 2011 to interview me for an article. This time I said, "yes." A short piece appeared in March 2012 along with profiles of other winners.

The typical journey for most famous people is fame, then fortune. But in my case, the money came first. The funny thing is I do not feel rich, though I should. And winning the Lotto is something to write about; though I honestly didn't consider it until my sister, Barb encouraged me. Winning isn't what I anticipated it to be. I imagined having all that money would make me happy for the rest of my life. It hasn't. Studies show that wealth and contentment go their separate ways after roughly $75,000 per year of income is realized. The research may be valid. Nevertheless, I know that I am happier than I would have been without the winnings.

I know now, *really* know now that having money doesn't assure happiness. I've come to realize that the elements, universally known for nurturing happiness such as good health, warm and supportive family and friends, are what really matters.

I'm the same person with the same strengths and weaknesses. Our family has its challenges. And believe it or not, there are some very real downsides of winning. Sometimes I feel more isolated than before I won.

What winning has given me is time and time is freedom. I could never have put the hours into writing my memoir if I had continued to work full-time. In addition, it's provided me with a ready-made story. As Al Franken writes in his book *Lies and the Lying Liars Who Tell Them: A Fair and Balanced Look at the Right*, no matter how dire the world situation is and the crises we face, people are always interested in lottery winners. I should know.

Some people are fascinated by the details. How did you find out? What were you doing? What was your reaction? What did you do? Well, I don't mind satisfying curiosity. Then, when your 15 minutes of fame are over, they're over. The fake check is relegated to the garage and no one cares after a while and why should they?

In his 2006 *Time* magazine essay, journalist and editor, Josh Tyrangiel remarks on Andy Warhol's prescience in his 1968 comment that "In the future everyone will be world famous for 15 minutes." What, one wonders; would Warhol have thought of how Facebook and YouTube have democratized fame? Yet while I've already had my 15 minutes, I long for another 15 or even 16.

To me it's not just the money, but it's the fame and recognition that are important. Obviously, I couldn't validate that until I *had* the fortune. Maybe that's why rich businessmen get the itch to run for public office.

In college, I had a few lifetime goals in mind. I was going to get married, become a doctor and have children, hopefully in that order. I should have been fulfilled and satisfied once I actually achieved this. However, I wanted more. I dreamed of being rich and famous.

I aspired to be like my late cousin Andrea Dworkin who was a rare breed among women. Andrea was known as a fierce intellectual feminist whose groundbreaking writings on pornography, violence against women and sexual politics inspired both intense admiration and unrelenting criticism. Her activism lit a generation with hope that their voices might be heard.

Although famous in literary circles, she was not rich by any means. I once joked with her that she was famous and I was rich and together we were "rich and famous." She had the right combo of fame; definite but not overwhelming.

It's a bit intimidating to set sail on a new career. In *Magical Thinking*, author Augusten Burroughs says he writes for eight hours a day, an impressive commitment. Oddly, Burroughs makes a reference to my cousin Andrea in the book. I was taken aback. I wonder what Andrea would think of falling into the pop culture realm.

Andrea was an inspiration to me in life and her death made me rise above my limitations. Her husband John Stoltenberg organized a memorial tribute. I spoke before the crowd of about 500, even though I am nervous speaking before even 10 people. It was the best speech of my life, if not the best speech given that day, and the competition was steep with Gloria Steinem, Robin Morgan and other luminaries giving remarks. However, I had an advantage knowing Andrea my whole life. I spoke from the heart and from childhood memories. As a radical feminist who denounced pornography, Andrea was a tough cookie on the outside. She didn't let her guard down to many although she did to me. After my address, my sister Barb, told me that it was perfect. Andrea would have been proud of me. I proved to myself that I can be successful at new things.

Still, professional writers must find it galling that so many of us think we can write. And nothing stops us poor souls from trying. I think many people yearned for careers as writers, actors, photographers and painters that they were too afraid to pursue since the financial rewards are precarious and the success rate is probably dismal. For example, I wanted to be a photographer at one point in my life but settled for it as a hobby. Seeking economic stability is a given if you grew up poor. When you attend medical or law school, you are virtually (how this word has changed over the last 20 years) guaranteed a job. While almost no one in mid-life can decide to become a doctor and practice medicine or law (although some people think they can represent themselves in court) many folks, including myself, think that they can embark on an encore career as a writer.

I have several friends that have written books and/or screenplays without success in getting them published.

Yet it is inspiring when success pops up among friends. Dr. Eva Ritvo, a psychiatrist friend co-wrote *The Beauty Prescription*, a self-help book. The authors got a lot of publicity including a segment on the TV show *Extra* and *The Today Show*. My friend Jill Bauer wrote *From I Do to I'll Sue*, a book on celebrity divorce published in 1993. Jill is now focused on documentary filmmaking. Her first movie *Sexy Baby* got accepted to the 2012 Tribeca Film Festival and we were there to cheer her on. The update on the movie *Sexy Baby* is that it is now a featured documentary shown on Showtime.

Pediatric emergency medicine is exciting and personally rewarding, but it won't get you famous. Sports, politics and the arts are where it's at. I do realize that most people in those fields work behind the scenes and are not known. But there's always the potential. Lots of doctors write books about their specialty, but there's limited potential for achieving fame with this genre unless you belong to the likes of Dr. Oz, Dr. Spock or Dr. Albert Schweitzer.

Can re-invention succeed? I can't help but recall Mark Poncy, with whom I conducted a research study some years ago. He later wrote and produced a musical that had some promise but closed quickly. I have to give him credit for trying though.

I saw the show just by happenstance. My friend Candace called me on a Friday and asked if I wanted to go to the theater in Hollywood, Fla. on Sunday.

"Yes," I said, though I had no idea what was playing. I rarely do anything spontaneously but this invitation seemed right. The play was called *Makeover*.

While reading the *Playbill* magazine at the theater, I noticed the playwright's name was Mark Poncy. Immediately I thought of the Mark Poncy I had worked with years earlier at the hospital. His medical equipment company had supplied pacifier thermometers for us to test in the Pedi-ER. I saw him about once a month during the yearlong project. We had established a rapport. Mark had told me he aspired to be a singer and gave me a CD he had produced. He also let me read a draft of his book *Manopause*.

After the project was complete, I never saw or heard from Mark again. From the research on the pacifier thermometer, Dr. Bruce Quinn and I co-authored a medical paper on the thermometer that was published in a premier medical journal. It was also noted in *The New York Times*. This article can be seen on my website (http://www.shirleypress.com) under Articles.

I looked up from reading the program and there was the same Mark. "You look familiar," he stated.

"Shirley Press from Jackson Memorial Hospital," I responded.

He said how nice it was to see me, but I wasn't sure he truly remembered me. He looked younger than he had 12 years before.

He found me again during intermission. He talked all about himself. I learned that he sold his company in 1997, published his book and wrote this musical titled *Makeover*. I felt a twinge of envy. He didn't ask me about my life. Even the simple question, "Are you still working at

Jackson?" would have been nice. He clearly didn't know about the lottery.

I mentioned I was writing. He proceeded to tell me that he hoped to write another book but his agent said there was no market for it. Later I was depressed that I had not pursued writing my book with the intensity needed. He did what he set out to do though he funded much of it himself. Trite, as it may seem, he followed his dream. The entire encounter left me encouraged but deflated. He had updated me on his children. Three went to Ivy League colleges and the fourth was pursuing a writing career. And he had nine grandchildren. He said that he must have done something right because all his kids were doing well. I run into this kind of naïve thinking all the time. He doesn't have a drug addict for a son.

Mark had achieved some local renown, but not real fame. I think of fame as falling into different categories. Kind of like that sampler cheese platter with seven selections or categories.

First, there are those famous for being famous **#1: Celebrity Fame**. On Feb. 8, 2007 Gershon and I were driving past the Seminole Hard Rock Hotel & Casino in Hollywood, Fla. Little did we know at that time paramedics were unsuccessfully trying to resuscitate Anna Nicole Smith. Her life was embroiled in controversy, but it was a fabulous life nonetheless. That kind of notoriety, whether considered fame or infamy, was not easy to achieve.

Journalists may have been perplexed that Anna Nicole's death was the day's top story. In my opinion, it was a top story because she was special – a real celebrity. Aside from being strikingly beautiful, her talents may be debatable. However, there was something engaging about her. Anna loved being famous and took enormous pleasure in her status.

She didn't seem to complain about an invasion of privacy. Many people say they don't want to be famous. I say baloney. Who wouldn't want to be? The proof of the matter to me is the thriving multi-million dollar publicity industry. Joel Stein wrote in *Time Magazine*, "We've found a group of people who are hot, rich and narcissistic to entertain us with their lives and another group to entertain us with their work." Anna Nicole Smith was definitely the former. To this category, we can add the Kardashian sisters who are an updated version of the Gabor sisters of yesteryear.

Many people thrive on attention. You see it with movie stars all the time. Career slump? He or she will accidentally on purpose do something outrageous. Or write a book with juicy details, like Jane Fonda confessing to being a part-time lesbian or Barbara Walters in her book *Audition* writing about her affair with then US Senator from Massachusetts, Edward Brooke. No matter how far they have gone in life they still felt a need to spruce up their stories. Then one could appear naked in a film àla former quarterback Terry Bradshaw in *Failure to Launch*.

But what can the average person do? Some dress or behave outlandishly. Others like me will venture outside their field of expertise. Psychopaths or the unstable commit crimes and sometimes actually document them. But most people simply live with quiet desperation that Thoreau described.

Then there's **#2: Accidental Fame**. Take Steven Slater, the Jet Blue flight attendant who became an overnight sensation after telling off a troublesome passenger and exiting his plane – and his anonymity – via the inflatable emergency chute. It's his one in a million chance for a celebrity career. Then there is Honey Boo Boo and her family who became overnight reality show sensations. That's the sheer randomness of life. Other examples of this include Sully Sullenberger, the US Airways pilot who landed the plane on the Hudson River on Jan. 15, 2009, and "Joe the Plumber," true name Joseph Wurzelbacher, who shot into the spotlight as an "everyman," after asking Senator Barack Obama a question during the 2008 presidential campaign.

Then there is **#3: Incidental Fame**, like Sarah Palin. She was known to few before Senator John McCain named the obscure governor as his 2008 running mate. Plucked from the heartland of Alaska and then – poof! She became the darling of the celebrity media long after mainstream political reporters moved on. Now she's known worldwide. She's all over the place. A recent search on Google shows more than 270 million references. Some people take a bit of attention and run with it. Kate Gosselin got noticed for having a houseful of kids and parlayed that into her TV show *John and Kate Plus Eight* and other venues, including books.

There are those who find **#4: Fame by Marriage**. Tipper Gore is an interesting woman. As a teen, she played drums in an all-girl band. She earned an advanced degree and worked as a newspaper photographer. By virtue of being married to the former vice president, she developed her own platform focused on mental illness treatment. The campaign to put mental illness on par with physical disabilities is probably her trademark. Could she have made such a difference without her husband? Who knows?

Of course, smarts and talent gain fame for many **#5: Fame for Talent**. I'd put Bill Maher in that category. I think *Real Time with Bill Maher* is in a league of its own. His guests include an array of politicians, writers, activists and actors. The show is sharp, funny, and it is clear that Bill is the real boss. Incidentally, my cousin Andrea would have been a great guest for his show. Entertainment, business and athletic talent are the royal road to fame for many. Take Norman Braman, a huge influence in the South Florida civic scene. But his renown isn't just from philanthropy and business savvy, but from owning the Philadelphia Eagles football team in the 1980s. Athletic fame lingers long after the action is over. Dr. Thompson, who took my place as the director of the Pedi-ER, was married to former NFL player Reyna Thompson. I asked her if he was still recognized. "All the time," she replied, noting that when their new plumber came to the house he first discussed football with her husband before turning his attention to their troublesome pipes.

Some people just seem to attract fame. Mia Farrow writes in her autobiography that when she and her sister Prudence went to India to meet the Maharishi they bumped into the Beatles (hence the song *Dear Prudence.*) And when she traveled to Thailand, she met Mother Teresa. Things like that just don't happen to most people.

Next are the recipients of **#6: Fleeting Fame**, the 15 minutes, and then it's over, for example Cindy Sheehan the Iraq anti-war activist. She was in the newspaper consistently for a while and then nothing.

Finally, there's **#7: One-Degree-of-Separation Fame**. It's interesting that I know a couple of people who have famous relatives. Our friend Barry Eichenbaum is first cousins with Judge Judy; my sister's friend, who I also know, is first cousins with attorney and author Alan Dershowitz. Of course, I am proud to say I have Andrea.

On the flip side, there are those that are more famous for their egregious behavior than they are for being in my seven fame categories. For example, there is Lance Armstrong whose call to fame is based on deceit and lying. If he didn't use steroids (doping), then he wouldn't have won his first Tour de France competition. He was cheating from the get-go and would have never achieved the enormous fame he encountered. And to take it a step further, if he weren't famous then he would have been a cancer survivor who most likely would not have received any media coverage.

There's also a hierarchy within fame. First, come the super über stars like Brad Pitt, Madonna, Beyoncé, Justin Bieber for now, Prince William and Kate, President and Michelle Obama, Bill and Hillary Clinton – all household names. The next level is the very famous like Robert de Niro, Meryl Streep, Barbara Walters or Pat Riley. Even super icons have an unofficial ranking. On the morning of June 25, 2009, Farrah Fawcett died after a courageous battle against anal cancer. But her death was almost immediately eclipsed by the avalanche of coverage for Michael Jackson's death that same afternoon.

This has happened before. Christopher Bonanos pointed out some amazing coincidences in a June, 2009 *New York* magazine feature *The Eclipsed Celebrity Death Club*. Princess Diana died on Aug. 31, 1997 and Mother Teresa on Sept 5, 1997. Groucho Marx's death on Aug. 19, 1977 was eclipsed by Elvis's death on Aug. 16, 1977. Dominick Dunne's death was overshadowed by Ted Kennedy's. However, the winners of the eclipsed death Olympics, according to Bonanos, go to Aldous Huxley and C. S. Lewis who both died on Nov. 22, 1963, the day President Kennedy was assassinated.

Conclusion: Fame is random.

One of my pet peeves is that many actors, athletes, and other celebrities aren't content with the fame they earn but enter into other fields, taking up even more than their share of space. Madonna branched out into writing children's books and has created her own fashion line. Swimmer Michael Phelps also wrote a children's book. The following actors all have rock bands: Joaquin Phoenix, Russell Crowe, Dennis Quaid, Bruce Willis, and Jack Black. The list goes on and on. How many struggling designers, writers and musicians do these celebrities displace?

It's just not fair, but that's the way it is. I'm not talking about stars like Oprah endorsing products and charities, which goes hand-in-hand with being a celebrity. I'm talking about trying to convince the public that they are multitalented.

There is a mystery to fame. Some of it is random; some of it is luck and some of it is talent. Many in the world believe it's all controlled by fate. A lot of it is perseverance. Sometimes it's a combination of factors like Al Gore. He is the son of a US Senator, well connected, extremely bright and hardworking. In his case, it's a snowball effect. Al took his advantages and made the most of them. (I once read about Al Gore's SATs and we had nearly the same score.)

Every now and then, I think back on my speech that I delivered at Andrea's memorial service in New York City on May 25, 2005 and I am encouraged.

ANDREA DWORKIN

I have known Andrea longer than most of the people in this room. I knew Andrea before she was famous. As a matter of fact, I have known her for all of 54 years. There was a reason for the longevity of our relationship: we were cousins. Aside from our familial heritage, we also had an enduring friendship.

Growing up in Camden, N.J., our families lived two blocks apart. I feel that it was her father Harry who was responsible for her and her brother Mark's brilliant intellect. And I am also sure that it was her mother Silvia who helped instill Andrea's fighting spirit. (Although Andrea would probably disagree with me on that.)

Sometimes she knew the odds were not in her favor, but it didn't stop her from advocating for the underdog. She cared deeply about people, especially those who suffered.

When other kids were out playing in the yard, my cousin Andrea was reading Malcolm X or D.H. Lawrence. Often times I would see her carrying books with titles and authors that were totally unfamiliar to me. That's because Andrea had a curiosity and inquisitiveness that belied her years. She was interested in the events of the Holocaust when no one else was. She asked my parents tirelessly about their concentration camp experiences, and often times wrote about my mother Leah in her books.

When I was 19 years old, our relationship changed. I knew that because she no longer allowed me to call her Andy as I always had. When I visited her in Amsterdam, she looked me straight in the eyes and said, 'Shirley, stop calling me Andy – I am Andrea.' It was at that moment I knew in my heart that my older cousin from Camden, New Jersey was going to lead a very special life. I think it was the defiant tone in her voice that gave me a hint that Andrea was destined for great things.

You see, my cousin always danced to her own beat. While my sister Barb and I were examining Mark's incredible bottle cap collection or playing marbles with him, Andrea would be reading in her room or playing the piano. To some Andrea was outrageous, but to me she was just my cousin with a kind heart and warmth, who I could talk to about anything. Andrea was not only loving and loyal, she was also funny.

Had we not have been cousins, I am sure that our paths would never have crossed. So I feel very lucky that they did. Andrea, I love you. I miss you. You'll always be in my heart.

Shirley Press

10. Help!

Winning the lottery was the biggest surprise of my life. Yet, there is no doubt about the worst shock of my married life -- when we realized Bill had only weeks, or even days, to live unless he underwent a liver transplant. It happened just as we were on the first leg of a long-planned vacation. Here is what I wrote a few days after Bill got sick.

August 2, 2008

It seems that everyone in my family needs me. I'm in New York. Our vacation plans have been derailed because Bill is sick. I was so looking forward to a summer vacation in Tanglewood with our friends Ron and Renee. So much for that. We spent 10 miserable hours in Weill Cornell Medical Center's ER (on Thursday, July 31). It is almost impossible to believe, but this facility was even more inefficient than Jackson's ER. Furthermore, I was dismissed as a nagging wife and not given the respect I deserve as a physician. Gershon is at home and I hope he doesn't relapse. I can't live my life never leaving home. My mother was looking forward to a couple of days with me in Cherry Hill, but five hours into the visit, Bill called moaning with excruciating pain. I had to ask the front desk of our apartment building in New York to call 911 since he wasn't able to move his spasm ridden body. So I immediately went back to the city, which took two hours by bus. Bill was in pain and nauseous.

The acuteness of the illness was scary; even though I knew from before we married that my husband had a continuing health issue. Bill, the middle son of June and Murray Rapoport's three boys, was 8 years old in 1957 when he became severely jaundiced. He was admitted to the hospital in Hartford, Conn., where the family lived. Doctors diagnosed him with hepatitis. Yet he continued to get worse.

Then a doctor friend said to Bill's father, "You know, Murray if this was my son, I'd have him transferred to Boston Children's Hospital."

After a few days in Boston, Dr. William Damashek diagnosed Bill with Wilson's disease, a genetic condition, in which a person's liver is unable to metabolize copper. In those days, the diagnosis was inevitably fatal; few with the condition ever reached adulthood. For many years, Bill was followed at Boston Children's by Dr. Huntington Porter, a child neurologist and an expert on Wilson's disease. At home, his parents had to inject him daily with painful shots of dimercaprol (also known as BAL) which eliminated his body's excess copper. He had to be on a special diet, avoiding foods such as nuts, seafood and some meats that have a high copper content. It must have been a frightful time for his parents, not knowing what his long-range prospects might be.

About a year after the initial diagnosis, Dr. Porter placed Bill on an experimental drug used in England called penicillamine, which was given in pill form. It saved Bill's life. This proved to be the definitive treatment for Wilson's disease and the US Food and Drug Administration approved it in 1963.

This new medication made Bill's disease almost a footnote, and things went back to normal for his family. Murray was involved in the community, leading various civic organizations. The boys were typical kids of the 50s and 60s. All had a Bar Mitzvah. All three as teenagers crashed cars.

Two of the boys followed in their father's footsteps, becoming optometrists, though Bill first considered a business career. To me, his disease was really incidental. Penicillamine meant he could live a normal life, though the pills caused some mild side effects over the years. And Bill always felt better in the warm weather.

After we moved to Florida, we lived a comfortable, uneventful life. We went to the movies, out to dinner and planned for our future. Bill was supportive of my residency. I remember once we were going out to eat and I was so tired that I fell asleep in the car on the way to the restaurant. Bill just quietly turned the car around. When I opened my eyes, we were back at the apartment. In addition, I've always appreciated Bill's willingness to listen. He was attentive to the kids when they were young, and close with Gershon, until our son began having problems in adolescence.

Then everything changed dramatically in August of 2008. I was already skirting a low point. The last four or five months had been a seesaw with Gershon. He had started using crack again in March which was a huge disappointment as he had been off drugs for more than a year. In April, he was arrested for violating a restraining order. But he had seemed to pull himself together and by the time Bill fell ill he had enrolled in welding school.

So I was looking forward to the New York respite. I always wanted to go on vacation with friends or family. Thank goodness for Judaism's Bar and Bat Mitzvah celebrations, which means people pretty much have to get together. But it had been a while since anything like that had come up. So Bill and I planned to join our friends for a Brandeis University seminar held near Tanglewood. However, the peace and quiet of the countryside were not to be.

After a series of tests and IV fluids, the ER docs discharged Bill, saying he was suffering from the effects of the Wilson's disease. But he soon got much worse.

August 4, 2008

Bill woke up yellow and swollen or in medical jargon jaundiced and edematous. Overnight this happened. Something is really wrong with him. He refuses to go back to the ER where he was seen Thursday and yesterday. I have spent the entire day trying to get my husband in to see a liver specialist. I am stuck in NYC... Occasionally, his disease will be the answer to a mysterious illness on a TV series like "House." Bill stopped seeing his liver specialist many years ago and therefore is no longer an active patient.

In truth, Bill had not been feeling well for months. A few years ago he had switched from seeing a liver specialist to being followed by our internist. As he had been stable for so many years, Bill decided continuing with the specialist was unnecessary. He had also switched from penicillamine to another medication. Moreover, everything seemed OK. Just a week earlier, his liver enzymes had come back fine.

August 4, 2008 (written later in the day)

Now he gets sick in NYC and without a physician to contact, it's a nightmare. No specialist would take him as a new patient since they are all so busy. Besides, it's August in New York and all the doctors are purportedly in the Hamptons at this time. However, one that does not take our insurance will see him. So off we go tomorrow. If he still had his liver specialist, one phone call could have probably gotten us an appointment. The lesson here - if you have a rare disease be followed by a specialist. Another lesson - always have a primary care physician where you live. Without one, you are also relegated to the ER.

My friend Mona lives here in Manhattan. I called her before I arrived in the city to make plans to get together, but she didn't call me back. I called her again today but still haven't heard back.

August 13, 2008

Bill saw Dr. Charles Maltz last week (Aug. 5th) who immediately admitted him to the hospital. My friend Mona called right back after I left an urgent message and then came to the hospital. It's been hell. Like you know it's bad when the hotdog guy at the hospital knows you already. After days of tests and having gallons of fluid called ascites drained from his (Bill's) abdomen, Dr. Maltz at Weill Cornell told us that Bill needed a liver transplant. We were in shock thinking that his liver failure could be controlled with a new medicine. Bill said there was no way he would undergo a transplant. So he was discharged with a prescription to try a new medicine.

It was clear that I had to get him back to Miami ASAP. We boarded a plane on Aug. 9. Bill was very jaundiced. His liver was failing and worst of all, he is mean when he does not feel well. This does not make him endearing to anyone especially me. I am stressed out of course.

He looked like a Chiquita banana. I wrote a note that he was not infectious in case he was going to be stopped by the airline personnel. But no one said or did anything about his appearance. Perhaps the world has learned to be politically correct. Many are afraid to ask. Alternatively, maybe no one noticed or gave a damn.

Once back in Miami, we saw Dr. Eugene Schiff, Bill's former hepatologist (liver specialist) at Jackson Memorial on Aug. 11, and we were given the bad news. Dr. Schiff agreed with Dr. Maltz that Bill needed an immediate transplant. He protested, but Dr. Schiff wouldn't hear any of it and immediately admitted him to the hospital for the liver transplant evaluation, tests and more drainage. Bill was supposed to be discharged home after a few days in the hospital to await the call that a matched liver was found. But he never left the hospital. He became critically ill waiting for the donor liver. There were times when I thought he would run out of time. As it turns out, he was days away from death. The liver transplant evaluation is an intense process. He went to the top of the list because his liver had deteriorated so fast. And just like on TV, a liver magically was found three to four days before Bill would have probably died.

I suspect people will think Bill went to the top of the list because I am a doctor, I work at Jackson Memorial Hospital and because we have money. However, that's not how the process works. The organ procurement agencies, which oversee donor-recipient matching, have a strict protocol. In general, patients who are the sickest get precedence and go to the top of the list especially those whose liver failure is due to genetic diseases, such as Bill's, those with acetaminophen (Tylenol) poisoning and those with acute rejection of a transplanted liver.

But the evaluation doesn't stop there. Doctors want to know that transplant recipients will care for the precious organ. Patients must demonstrate that they are prepared to comply with the necessary regime of medications and follow-up tests. It certainly helps if one has a stable home life. If I did have an edge, it was in knowing what factors would be looked at.

The evaluation includes a psychiatrist's visit. It just so happened that my computer was on, showing a photo of our family, when the doctor came in the room. She commented on it. I presented our family in the very best light and I think the psychiatrist liked us. This is one more piece of advice – put your best foot forward when being evaluated for something scarce.

August 21, 2008

Bill underwent a liver transplant today. I am curiously detached. I cried for the last two weeks when I thought about the possibility of his dying. Yet today, as he was rolled into the operating room, I was unemotional, perhaps from exhaustion. He has been so difficult these last weeks as his liver was failing. I felt really bad for him since he was suffering so much. You expect to take care of a sick child or a sick parent, yet a spouse is different. To see Bill so emaciated and weak has affected me negatively. How can this man near death return, if ever, to the role of a strong husband? Will I see him as weak forever? I have ambivalent feelings. These weeks have robbed me of most of my personal time. I know I'm being selfish, but it's the way I feel.

June, my mother-in-law, stayed with me. She was very helpful to Bill, and sat with him for days on end at the hospital, allowing me to take occasional breaks and attend to other things. I was grateful for June's help. Still, there were fears and emotions I couldn't share with her. So my anxieties bubbled along underneath. What would happen if Bill didn't recover? Or became an invalid? Being a doctor didn't make one bit of difference when it came to facing the ups and downs of a severe illness in the family.

September 4, 2008

On 8/21, just after midnight we were notified about a possible matched liver donor. Bill was transferred to Jackson from the University of Miami Hospital across the street. Initially, we were told that if the liver was a good match, the surgery would take place around 4 a.m. By 9 a.m. we were abandoning hope, but despite unforeseen delays, it turned out to be the right match. Bill went into surgery for his liver transplant at noon that day. The twelve hour surgery was performed by Dr. David Levi and his team. We all had been up for 30 hours straight. It felt like being an intern again. The surgery went well; Bill spent five days in the ICU and then was transferred to the transplant floor where he stayed another six days. In total with the New York hospital stay, he spent 25 days in the hospital. Bill's life was saved for the second time. He was discharged on 13 different medications including insulin. He was very weak and in a lot of pain. Sarah flew back from NYC and then returned when the crisis was over.

Bill's brothers, Michael and Steven, came to visit, and Gershon did also, though their relationship was still strained. Gershon relapsed that October and dropped out of trade school. At least though, he was all right during Bill's worst days.

September 8, 2008

I am going through the antithesis of my Lotto experience. Now, I ask: how many people does this happen to? Well, actually the prevalence of Wilson's disease is 1 in 30,000. The probability of needing a liver transplant with this disease is less than 5 percent. So if you multiply 30,000 times 1-in-20, the odds are that someone has both Wilson's disease and has undergone a liver transplant are approximately one in 600,000 or greater. Not quite the odds of the Lotto win but still, rare enough. This is admittedly an exercise in futility since it doesn't matter what the statistics are when it happens to you.

Looking back, I recall some of my random thoughts of those days with absolute clarity, though so much else remains hazy. Over the years ragging about my hospital had become my pastime. I remember wondering whether I could still complain about Jackson after the hospital had saved my husband's life.

September 11, 2008

I've lost six weeks plus of my life to Bill's liver failure and transplant. It's been quite an ordeal. It is really a miracle to have a stranger's liver transplanted into you. Bill and I both remember that the donor in death made the most generous of gifts. We are celebrating when another family is mourning. Yesterday, which was the seventh anniversary of my Lotto win, was the first day that I had lunch with a friend since July. Actually, it seems as if I have always been a Lotto winner. My desk is an absolute mess and my days are filled with 15-20 chores each day. It's now 12:41 a.m. and I absolutely must wash my hair and work on my investment club reports. There's more and more responsibility with Gershon, Bill and me. I was going to go to court and fight my traffic ticket for speeding, but who has time? So I paid a "ticket clinic" to handle it for me.

We were told that the donor was middle-aged and died in a car accident. His liver was his extraordinary last gift, and to a stranger no less. Bill wrote a beautiful letter to the donor's family expressing gratitude for the man's generous soul. The message was sent through the transplant center as donor families and recipients are not allowed to meet or even know much about one another. We never heard back from the family.

The first months back at home were very stressful. Bill didn't want a nurse, so I injected him with the insulin he needed during those first weeks while his body was adjusting to the new liver. June remained with us for some time. Then we sent her home and just struggled along.

After something unusual happens in your life and you think it may be a rare occurrence, you usually meet others who have experienced what you've gone through, maybe not winning the Lotto, but for other events. After we adopted our son, I was barraged by people coming up to me with their own adoption stories.

Then, after I had appendicitis at age 40, which is rare, I met a handful of people who had also gone through this in middle age. The folks at work couldn't get enough of the fact that a pediatric emergency doctor in her own life was subjected to what is, usually, a pediatric emergency. Oh, the irony of it all.

We actually met one other person who also went through a liver transplant. Yet most of the stories were secondhand or had degrees of separation. People knew of someone who knew someone who had gone through a liver transplant. Then liver transplants became high profile when it leaked out that Apple Computer's founder Steve Jobs had a liver transplant. When a celebrity goes through something like this, headlines usually make it seem seamless. The celebrity claims to be "good as new" in just a couple of months. Yet most won't reveal how awful the experience truly was.

Maybe that's changing. Bill Clinton spoke of how hard his recovery from bypass surgery was. Farrah Fawcett made her documentary *Farrah's Story* to record her pain and suffering for the world. I think this trend is good and refreshing.

Many people don't understand the gravity of a liver transplant. Well-meaning friends and acquaintances would come up to me and say, "Oh, my brother had a kidney transplant and he's doing great." But a kidney isn't a liver.

As an organ, the liver, with its many functions, is much more complicated than a kidney. It has a larger, complex blood supply and so the operation takes much longer than does a kidney transplant. Recovery is slower.

In addition, it is psychologically different. If a kidney fails, a person can go on dialysis, at least for a while. But there is nothing to replace a liver. If it fails and there is no donor, the person dies. That fact weighed on us and still does. When Bill woke up jaundiced a few months after the transplant, we feared the worst. He had to be re-hospitalized twice during the first six months but it wasn't rejection.

It took Bill months to regain the 30 pounds he lost. At one time, we were within 10 pounds of each other. He had a lot of pain and sometimes vomited. But things slowly and steadily improved.

Bill has yet to regain all his energy, but he has come a long way. I knew when he started cleaning again that he was feeling better. My husband is like Felix in *The Odd Couple.*

It was late October, two months after the transplant, when we ventured out for our first big event. It was a birthday party for 20 people thrown by my friend, Dr. Margie Duarte, at the former Versace mansion on South Beach. It was a cool affair and a nice way to mark Bill's return to socializing with friends.

Bill stopped practicing optometry in 2003, a year after my lottery win. It made sense. His job had also become routine. There wasn't a need to continue his practice. Instead, he took on the chore of tracking our finances. That can eat up hours each day. Even with our financial advisor overseeing our portfolio, we must also continually study investments. Bill became president of our condo association, a post he held for two years. And, as it turns out, he would not have been able to work anyway after his liver transplant due to his chronic fatigue.

I often felt sorry for him. I felt sorry for myself too. I was angry about having a husband and a son with serious health conditions. It's draining. But families must also adjust to the challenges a medical condition brings. It was really no accident that I began writing my book around this time. I've always had diaries, but now I began shaping them into chapters. Late at night was, and is, one of my favorite times to write.

Late one evening Bill finally asked me what I was typing.

"Nothing," I responded.

He persisted.

"I'm writing my memoir," I relented.

He laughed and said that someone already wrote *The Diary of a Mad Housewife.* Well, at least his sense of humor was back.

He asked me if I had affairs to reveal. "No," I said.

Consequently, he said, "You have nothing interesting to write about."

"Well, we'll see about that," I responded. I think he's a bit jealous.

"You're using my transplant as material."

I joked and said, "Now if you *hadn't* made it, *that* would be a better story."

Yet it's true that the scare drew us closer, at least for a while. In the midst of the crisis and during its immediate aftermath we appreciated each other more. Bill was grateful for my help and support. And I realized how much I rely on him. Yet eventually we went back to our same old selves. Now I'm grumbling about his obsessive neatness and he complains about how much time I spend on the book and at the local casinos. If that's not the definition of "back to normal," I don't know what is.

Bill needs to have medical tests every month. We schedule those tests without fail, even if we happen to be in New York at the time and must have them done in the city. We know that we've been so very lucky.

One year after the surgery, Bill's 60th birthday was a celebration of life. We had dinner at the Capital Grill with his family and a few friends. Below is the poem I wrote for the occasion.

October 3, 2009

To Bill:

Don't worry a bit about turning the big six-o
You're young at heart and in the know
So in this poem I'll offer a rendition
Of your life, after all, poems are my tradition

It all began way back when
Harry S. Truman was president then
Born in Hartford to June and Murray
Brothers Michael and Steven make it five in a hurry

You spent your youth in Connecticut
And then studied at UM to avoid the winter's rut
Then returned to school in the City of Brotherly Love
When we met, something seemed right from the sky above

We then moved to Miami Beach after we finished school
You became an optometrist who also enjoyed the pool
And then in one blessed year of elation
Came Gershon and Sarah which ended relaxation

You're a great father and a wonderful spouse
Who takes pride in maintaining the cars and the house
Where a speck of dust just can't hide
I'd still choose you to be by my side

You are a special husband, father, son, brother, uncle, cousin and
friend
Who is loyal to the very end
Yes, Bill is made of the right stuff
He survived when times were tough

A year ago we almost lost you
A miracle happened and you are anew

Shirley Press

I know I'm lucky to have a guy so nifty
As your family and friends celebrate your birthday at sixty!
All my love, Shirley

11. With a Little Help From My Friends

Friends are tough. I think, how can anyone honestly be happy for you when you've won the lottery? I might have to settle for those who begrudge me the least. How do you know who your true friends are after you've won the lottery? Easy. At some point, they insist on going back to splitting the check. OK, that's a bit of an inside joke between Bill and myself.

People say being down and out reveals friends in their true light. How about when everything is coming up roses and you are in the money? That's also when you find out what those who share your confidences are made of. Ours ran the gamut. Most of our friends, like Lisa and Barry Eichenbaum - our close friends for 25 years - took it in stride and helped us through the adjustment period, realizing that even happy changes aren't so easy. It's really comforting to have old friends like them.

We kept much of the upheaval to ourselves. Who really wants to hear exhaustive details about dealing with a windfall? Take it from someone who had never before heard of a private bank before. However, I was able to confide in my family. My sister Barb is my forever, best friend.

She listens when others wouldn't have the patience. Cousins Bev and Janet are also great confidants. I can call all of them with any emotion I am feeling: from tears to hysterical laughter.

For months we insisted on picking up the tab at every outing with friends. Finally, most of our friends made us stop, and we went back to taking turns or splitting the check. It was a welcome return to normalcy. We could be ourselves again.

I have always strived for acceptance by others. It's a thirst for reassurance. I sometimes would compromise myself to get into someone's favor. Even as an adult, I would go out of my way to do something nice for someone even when it was never acknowledged or reciprocated. The lottery has freed me of that (ass-kissing) for the most part. I have become more true to myself. Adjectives I would use to describe myself are sensitive, loyal, organized, balanced and trustworthy. I shouldn't have to be obsequious.

Some people would be jealous of a friend's lottery win. I admit, I would be too. It would probably fall into that mixed emotions category - happy for them and sad that it didn't happen to me. I expect that is the most common reaction. However, for some friends the money became a barrier they couldn't get over; like a competition they didn't win. Connie was exhibit "A."

Only friends or relatives can ease the heartache of sitting with a sick husband wondering if he will ever get well. That's how I felt during the weeks before and after Bill's liver transplant. We were lucky a donor liver was found in time. But it was a low point made even lower when Connie, who I'd considered one of my best friends, never came to see Bill, though I had often visited her parents when they were in the hospital. Granted, her father died when Bill was hospitalized, but she still had months to visit him at our house. Instead, her husband came as her representative. I never confronted her about this. There were much more relevant issues to deal with like Bill's health.

What really stung was that if her husband had been seriously ill, I surely would have visited him. She called but that wasn't enough for me. Yet, after analyzing this to death (sorry about the pun) I wasn't that surprised. I had already begun to think of my friendship with Connie as a casualty of the lottery. The drawn out disintegration of the friendship was a gnawing feeling that I had felt for years after the lottery win in 2001.

"What happened with her?" I asked a mutual friend after the fourth time Connie had let me down.

"She is really jealous of your win," my friend replied.

Then I heard that from another and another. I guess I was being punished. Things were fine with Connie when I was her fan, the second fiddle, the follower. We would talk for hours and I truly enjoyed our friendship. We confided in each other. We did things together. Our minds were in sync. She was sharp and analytical as I fancy myself to be on occasion. In spite of that, I took on the role of the deferential one and to be honest I did not mind it. Connie is slender and striking and enjoys all the attention her appearance courts. She is also a high-achieving professional. She and her husband are well off and their children and grandchildren turned out fine. Her life was an apparent success and I gravitated to her.

Looking back, I realized Connie often made negative comments about other people. In fact, she related to me an incident where a friend said something off-putting to her. Connie's response was to expediently end the friendship. I was afraid she would do that to me. I felt the closeness slipping away but I did not want to lose her as a friend. So I never talked to her about the things that she did against me. I am aware that it's illogical. What kind of friend was she if I began feeling I couldn't really talk to her about the things that were bothering me? But, it is emotional and irrational. Things with time would get better I told myself. Just hang in there. *Keep on truckin. The close bonds will be renewed.* However, that didn't happen. The whole thing reminds me of the competitive women of *The Real Housewives of New York City* TV show or the movie *Mean Girls*, which portrays the backstabbing, gossip and manipulation that seems to occur in female friendships. It seems more like a rivalry than a friendship.

I think it was the self-confidence I gained post lottery and not only the money that upset Connie. For the first time in my life, I was really able to do what I wanted. Moreover, I was doing it: writing, traveling, working by choice, becoming more active in charities and joining investment and writers groups. She could not accept my expanded self.

But losing her friendship was painful. We were buddies for more than two decades, attended the milestone celebrations for each others' children, commiserated about life in general, elderly parents, being middle aged and, I thought, cheered on each others' success. Looking back, I see the fissures in our friendship were always there.

In 2006, Connie started canceling plans we made as a foursome with our husbands. Still, I kept up the girlfriend part. Then she began to leave me out of her life. She stopped confiding in me. Our conversations were stunted. I was calling her more. The reciprocity that had been there all along was going downhill. Then she started canceling lunches. She did not invite me to her house anymore. Even when I realized the friendship was over, absurdly, I hung on for another three years. The last straw was when she excluded me from her inner circle and didn't share an important life event. It was over. Now what do I do with all of the photos of us together? What happens with the secrets after a friendship ends? Morally, I feel I must still keep her confidences.

I see echoes of her most irritating traits – jealousy and social climbing in myself though I try not to be like that. What a mean girl mess. It's very junior high yet it persists even into old age. My mother now lives in a senior complex where she is sometimes shut out of some dinner tables because they are "full." Some of these women are friends she has known for more than 50 years. Who knows why?

At first, I wanted her to apologize to me but that didn't happen. So Connie and I have never reconciled. The only good thing to come out of my breakup with Connie is that it galvanized me to seek out new friends.

"If Connie had been a sister or a cousin," I said to Barb when we were discussing the issue, "we would feel pressured to bring our family together again."

There is no question the lottery can complicate both old and new friendships. It took a year for me to tell my oldest friend Marsha about the win. That was because at the same time, her sister had been diagnosed with a serious illness. Finally, I had to.

"I have something to tell you," I said. "You won't believe this; I won the Florida lottery."

"Oh my God, that's great, that's great," she exclaimed. But she was puzzled when I told her it was past a year. "Why didn't you tell me sooner?" she asked.

"How could I when your sister was sick?" I replied.

There are friends I still haven't told. It can become a stress test. You instantly know whether jealousy will corrode a relationship. I also don't bring it up when I meet someone new. Think about it. How often does the subject of lotteries come up in a conversation anyway? I want people to like me for myself and not because I am a lottery winner. I sometimes wait years to mention it.

It wasn't until I stepped down from the Pedi-ER directorship that I began to think more about my friendships. Until then, I'd had close friends, but work and the family kept me too busy. Bill is my biggest supporter, friend and sounding board. For many women, a husband is enough. But to me a husband is not the same as a girlfriend.

I had more time for friends after the lottery and I began analyzing some of the friendships which I don't recommend. Just go with the flow is better in the long run. But that's not me and I began looking critically at several friendships. Does the friend call me or do I call? Do they give me the attention I give them or am I being squeezed in? Is there reciprocity? On and on, I would analyze, scrutinize and dissect. I know this is unhealthy for me and I have to stop this.

Maybe I should have just listened to my mother who always said, "If you drop a friend because they do something you don't like, then you will have no friends left."

Perhaps I expected too much. I confess that popularity or recognition is important to me. And that, I know, is ridiculous even at my age. I don't know, but it is what it is. At times, I feel very alone.

I long for a group of all-purpose friends like those assembled on *Seinfeld, The Mary Tyler Moore Show, Sex and the City*, or *Friends* where people are in touch everyday and are always there for you. Is this some sort of TV fantasy? Alternatively, is it adolescence taken into adulthood? In high school, I'd see my friends Marsha and Ann daily and later, on the phone, we'd microanalyze the day's events for hours. I don't have that now.

I guess that's what Facebook and other social networking sites try to replicate and expand on; like the telephone was in my day. Some people "friend" hundreds on their Facebook pages. Lots of folks don't even know who their "friends" are. Meanwhile, though Facebook was created by and tailored for college kids, it has become the baby boomers' de facto connection to the 50s, 60s and 70s. You can find people from venues such as elementary school, junior high, high school, Hebrew School, camp and college. Organizers for my 40th high school reunion used Facebook to communicate with classmates.

I joined Facebook in April 2009 and I now have 400 friends. I was curious. I found and then wrote to a guy from high school who I dated twice. I had the biggest crush on him thinking he was the coolest guy on earth. He was cute and I considered him a rock music guru. We weren't a good match. He wanted someone "fast" and that wasn't me although he tried to convince me otherwise. He and his family moved away but he continued to write me love letters until the relationship finally faded. Well, you guessed it. He didn't remember me at all. And he's fat and bald to boot. He wrote back that my name sounded vaguely familiar. What are you going to do? Without the Internet, I wouldn't have received this virtual rejection.

Yet it's hard to form the kind of close bonds in adulthood as we did as kids. Everyone is busy. Staying near your childhood community helps preserve ties. I grew up in Camden, New Jersey. No one I know still lives there. Many, like my sister and brother-in-law, moved to the nearby suburbs. They have roots. Having moved hundreds of miles away from my hometown, I feel I have no roots except if we're talking hair.

Too often adult friendships are built around just one or two activities, such as going out to lunch or work. I think of this as "Friends in a

Vacuum." Friends only know me and not my family or other friends and vice versa. How would we find out if something happened to one another?

Still, you have to ask, is it even possible to have circles of friends in real, adult life? I have in mind something like ABC's *The View*. I often meet with women for lunch or dinner. At times, our conversations prove as interesting as Barbara Walters and her gang talking over a vast array of topics in a living room setting. We are sharp, witty and entertaining. My friends and I adopted the sobriquet of *The Unknown View* for ourselves. Maybe we should call it *The Unseen View*.

Experience has taught me a few friendship "rules." I usually am not close friends with people who have lived in my area all their lives. They are generally integrated in the community and already have enduring childhood friendships. Lori and Stephanie are exceptions to this "rule" and are close friends. If the other person is too cultured or sophisticated and I feel out of my league, just forget it. Age differences sometimes hamper closeness. Cultural differences can be a barrier. When I refer to *Rocky and Bullwinkle*, I want people to know what I'm talking about. However, I ignore these guidelines if exceptional people come my way.

Other things I've learned along the way. Some friendships have expiration dates such as when someone gets married or moves away. For example, I had a friend Tammy. We shared exercising, lunches and trips to the casinos. She met and married the love of her life and moved away. She didn't go that far, but she was swept into a new social scene and I realized our friendship had run its course. It's ironic that what was good for her was bad for me because I miss her. Other times you can develop a friendship with someone who is working on a project with you. Then sometimes when the project is over, so is the situational friendship.

Furthermore, I have become very cautious about one-sided friendship when I feel I'm making all the effort. I don't want to be fit in. I want to *be* the agenda. I shouldn't have to try so hard. The lack of self-confidence that many shy people like me suffer from has probably kept me working at friendships longer than I should have.

I can't help but think of Jackie. This is an example of what I call an uneven or unbalanced friendship. Yet my experience with her taught me an invaluable lesson. Don't push it. For new friendships I don't go overboard calling. I let a natural rhythm of bonding occur and if it doesn't happen, there is no more to do.

Jackie was not jealous of my money or professional achievements. She's a brilliant conversationalist. For years, every lunch was like *My Dinner with Andre*, a feast of ideas, stories and psychological insights.

I met Jackie about a year before I won the lottery. She's older than me. I found her to be intimidating, aloof, and paradoxically, one of the most insightful people I've ever come across. She was like the mentor I never had in high school or college, a Morrie Schwartz to my Mitch Albom from the bestseller *Tuesdays with Morrie*.

Over the years, we had more than 60 lunches. Our conversations have left me elated and enchanted but also feeling taken for granted because I never knew where I stood with her. Why is she so remarkable? For Jackie, success is a reflection of power. She's comfortable being cool and dismissive which I found intriguing.

I remember that our first lunch was good and the conversation flowed. She was exciting and interesting and to my relief did almost all of the talking. She talked for at least an hour and a half straight about herself, her politics and her views. My only contribution that I recall was relaying that sometimes adopted girls subconsciously imitate their birth mothers and become pregnant in their teens.

I was thrilled when she asked if we could have lunch again.

"Sure," I replied.

But, I didn't hear from her. I decided to fax her an essay on George W. Bush being the recipient of elitist affirmative action. Alas, no response. I finally called her twice and left messages. A few weeks passed and I had given up. Then she called.

"Would you like to have lunch again?" I asked.

There was a long pause – then an affirmative response. That set the pattern of an emotional roller coaster and a preview of what I would encounter. We would have lunch once a month. I would mostly listen, occasionally sharing parts of my life. But I never knew if each lunch would be the last. I let her disparaging statements roll off my back. I just couldn't tell if she liked me or if I was just a sounding board. I tried not to have any expectations. At each lunch I felt like I was auditioning for the next one. Was I interesting or witty enough? I felt like she didn't appreciate or need me in her life.

Each lunch was a free-for-all of ideas and topics. At first, I was usually the listener urging her to go on with her thoughts and opinions. But eventually, I began to contribute more to the conversation and spoke up when my view was contrary to hers. Sometimes she was annoyed, sometimes not.

Two years into our friendship we met for lunch after we both returned from significant trips. She had traveled around the world. I had gone to Eastern Europe and seen Auschwitz and other concentration camps, the mission of a lifetime. She told me about her trip. I told her about mine and showed her pictures. She was uncomfortable. She finally asked me a personal question. Why had I gone to the camps? I told her that my parents were Holocaust survivors, a circumstance that has a crucial impact on my life. She was shocked. I don't know if she was taken aback because they were survivors or that all this time she had never asked about my childhood.

I told her in detail that my mother was a teenage survivor of Auschwitz and my father a survivor of Dachau. She was astonished. Our lives could not have been more different, which I had long before realized. They were, in fact, diametrically opposite – American vs. foreign parents, intellectual vs. pragmatic, rich upbringing vs. poor childhood, educated in elite schools vs. scholarship kid. Yet I knew she might have the capacity to understand.

Then I'm sitting there and was absolutely flabbergasted when Jackie pontificated like she was giving a lecture on the Holocaust in her most professorial manner. She sounded off that the Holocaust was not just a Jewish event, but a universal event. I sat there so shocked that I didn't remember anything else. What she said may be true – the Holocaust permanently changed the world. But for me it is not a jumping off point for abstract discussion. It's overwhelmingly personal. Instead of choosing empathy for the fact that my parents' sibling and parents and many other of our relatives were exterminated by the Nazis, Jackie retreated to intellectualism and distance. I wanted to scream and cry.

That night I called Andrea Dworkin, my cousin, for insight. She listened intently. She had been through this. She told me that if a woman she liked didn't share her views on rape, pornography and the abuse of women, she didn't get involved no matter how much she initially thought she was interested in the person. After that, my friendship with Jackie lost some of its intensity. I realized that she was never going to provide the warmth or reassurance I was seeking. Yet we remained friends. I found that I was taking my mother's advice after all, and accepting Jackie for who she was. I took a long time to call her again. Yes, I did all the calling. When we met the next time she knew in her own way that I was disappointed in her and she did try to assure me that she had empathy for survivors.

We, I felt, had reached an equilibrium. At the beginning of our friendship, I felt I could only reveal little pieces of myself since we were so different. And I feared rejection. Over and over I felt rebuffed by her but hung on anyway. But I finally became myself and not just an agreeable fan. I have learned that unbalanced relationships don't work for me. Things had to change. I pulled back and stopped calling. She started to call me, which I was pleased about. I thought the friendship was finally working on some levels. Unfortunately for me (at the time), our friendship had a sad and sudden ending.

In the spring of 2010, at my last lunch with Jackie, which I didn't know was going to be our last lunch, I brought up the subject of this book, which I had previously mentioned. I told her that I had written about her and she said, with false modesty, that she didn't think there was anything about her to warrant a story. Still, she seemed flattered. Then I gave her the caveat that she might not like everything I wrote.

"Don't worry," she responded with typical Jackie bravado, "I can take a little disparagement. In fact, you can disparage me all you want."

I felt relieved and stupidly believed her. She seemed tough enough. If she had objected to being in my book, I would have just taken out the pages about her and our friendship would have just continued. After all the years of her controlling behavior of never calling me, never offering to drive the 56 miles round-trip and her condescending comments, I felt reassured that our friendship rested, at long last, on a firm foundation. I was wrong.

A few weeks after our lunch, a mutual acquaintance relayed to Jackie a sensationalized account of what I had written about our friendship. Jackie asked me about this and I volunteered to send her what I had written. I quickly – too quickly – emailed the parts I had written about her. Momentarily, I thought that she would find it interesting or at the very least thought-provoking. Yet a second after the click, I had that awful sinking feeling that she would be offended, no matter what she said at lunch. Then I thought, we could talk it over and I would revise the piece.

That didn't happen. Her ego couldn't take it. I called her a number of times. I emailed her as well. No response. Nothing. She never spoke to me again.

In the weeks following, I felt really bad. Yet I also had a nagging feeling of déjà vu, another time that a bruised ego ended a connection, but I couldn't place it. Then I recalled my residency and Dr. N. He was the pediatrician who never spoke to me again after I suspected a problem that he missed in baby Timmy. Yes, I've been there, done that. Jackie was Dr. N. all over again.

As I was finishing the last chapters of my book, I saw the documentary *Joan Rivers: A Piece of Work*. The film, covering both her personal and her show biz life, is fast paced, entertaining and revealing. One story jumped out at me. It was about how the *Tonight Show's* host, Johnny Carson, who often tapped Rivers as guest host, cut off all contact after she accepted a proposal for her own late-night talk show. Each of them felt betrayed by one another.

I never really cared about Dr. N. going his own way. But the crazy thing is, with Jackie, I still miss her. I always cherished her friendship, despite everything. I hope someday we will reconnect. Then I remind myself that Johnny Carson and Joan Rivers never reunited. I'm beginning to think: is this a universal theme? I guess Jackie felt betrayed by me but I also felt that way. She insisted that she was such a resilient and open-minded person that I thought she was flexible enough to see that this was an homage to her, albeit, in an odd kind of way.

The need to be wanted or feel important is so basic. I've found it to be one way to move past my shyness. So it's always been a theme in my life, and in my friendships. I help others. But sometimes it's not reciprocated. That became clear to me after my June 2008 shoulder surgery. I was in pain and feeling sorry for myself. I'm the one who always visits people when they are sick or in the hospital and I also go to a lot of funerals to show support. I kept thinking about Dale Carnegie's book *How to Win Friends & Influence People*. He emphasizes that you should never criticize anyone. Is that realistic? I couldn't help but be hurt by those who didn't call me after my surgery.

Then I went to a Hadassah meeting where the featured speaker was a woman who promotes herself as a happiness coach. She trained under a "happiness professor" from a top university and has fashioned herself as a motivational speaker and business consultant. The premise is that if your workforce is happy, your business will thrive. Her message is to look for the positives in everything. After the lecture, I bumped into her and said I enjoyed her talk. She asked me about my sling. I told her of my surgery.

Her response: "Think of something positive that has to do with your surgery."

I stood there silent.

She then repeated herself, imploring, "There must be something."

So to satisfy her I said, "A lot of people have called to see how I'm doing."

"There's the positive," she said and seemed relieved.

I just didn't want to upset her. Another *Curb Your Enthusiasm* episode. It's hard to put a positive spin on everything because there are some categories where this can't be done like the Holocaust, drug addiction and death.

As we age, my generation is already learning how important friendships are. I realize I'm not alone in feeling lonely. A 2013 *New York Times* article reported on studies showing that the rate of suicide jumped 40 percent in whites who are 35 to 64 years old.

While some researchers were baffled, others said it was likely due to flimsy support networks and the result of frequent moves, often away from family and close friends. Hell, you could have just asked me. That is the age when you realize that there's probably not more to life than what you are already experiencing.

Friendships change for many reasons. People forget. Society is impersonal and everyone is so busy. It's even more lonely when you're sick, can't drive and friends don't visit. That's why widowhood is so bad. It's rated the number one stress inducer because it's so lonely.

When I turned 50, I was very depressed with the realization that I was never going to be rich or famous. While, circumstances like the Florida Lotto made me rich, I am still struggling to be known. So I'm "rich and un-famous." And I will be sure to take my friends along for the ride if the fame ever comes along.

In the years since the lottery win, I've tried to assemble a support system of people who like me for myself and reciprocate my interest in friendship. Before Bill got sick, I had begun by organizing dinners out with couples that we know. The couples jelled and got to know each other. That came to halt because of the transplant, but now I'm considering resurrecting it – making blind reservations for 10 to 12 people and filling it up. Maybe it's not *The View, Seinfeld* or *Friends* but something more like *Friends with Shirley.*

12. A Day in the Life

I have always tracked my life. I have kept my calendars from 1974 to the present time where I can go back and examine my life if I want to do that. It actually helped to have kept those calendars to verify dates and incidences of my life to be as accurate as possible in writing this book. Besides the calendars, I have 30 filled to the brim photo albums not counting the ones at my mother's home. I also made scrapbooks for Gershon and Sarah. And I have three large boxes of stuff from my childhood to review more thoroughly. I was Facebook before Facebook.

The lottery has given me time to think and think and think. It has also given me a unique identity. Now I acknowledge that everyone is unique but being a lottery winner is really something else. With just three factors – I am distinctive. Being a 1 in a 20 million winner, being the daughter of Holocaust survivors and being left handed (one in ten persons) accomplishes this task.

Like most, I have a daily routine. I make the bed first thing which gives me a sense of order for the day. I then write down early morning thoughts and dreams. I've learned that some of these remembrances are fleeting and later in the day I can't remember them. After applying sunscreen and makeup to make myself look natural, I go downstairs and have orange juice and an Oreo or Lorne Doone cookie for breakfast. When I don't have to go to work, I spend my day running errands, reading, writing, shopping, having lunch with friends, going to the casino, working on the computer, watching TV, preparing meals, gardening and doing nothing special as my mind mentally wanders. The word for this is puttering and I know it is a luxury to sit and think about nothing. Every evening that I am home I watch *Jeopardy*. My performance is erratic. For the most part, I clobber the contestants. Then on other nights – not so good. Sometimes I like to just veg out and watch TLC, HGTV or some sitcoms. I also enjoy watching classic movies on television such as *Casablanca* which is my all time favorite movie as well as my father's. Bill and I eat out about two nights a week. If we went out every night then it wouldn't be special. We also argue a lot about money: how to invest, where to donate and who do we help out. Yes, this is a negative side effect of the lottery.

One of the things I most enjoy doing is having analytical, clever, stimulating conversations with friends and characters that cross my path. A lot of people prefer email and texting but not me. There is no way to intensively engage except by real talking. I read a lot of magazines and journals each week including my medical journals, *Time Magazine*, *New York Magazine*, *TV Guide*, investment magazines and various publications from organizations and charities. I read a book a month. The most influential book to affect me personally has got to be *The Sociopath Next Door* by Martha Stout, Ph. D. I now have my radar up for sociopaths (those without a conscience) who seem to pop into my life.

At times, I am the person who writes to companies pointing out omissions or just complaining. For example, I have written twice to the Lego Company pointing out that the little pieces in their store bins are choking hazards. Yes, there are warning signs posted but I wrote that this is not good enough. They insist that their stores are safe for children and that their personnel monitor the areas. I still disagree.

Years ago I wrote to the McArthur Dairy indicating the lack of life preservers in a row boat featured in one of their commercials. They wrote back thanking me and said the commercial was not going to run any more. I've complained about long lines, dirty stores and rude employees. Most of the time, I get responses. Walmart is an exception. I wrote twice about their having bumpers in their crib ads. Bumpers are unsafe for babies and should not be used anymore. No response either time.

Being a lottery winner does not excuse me from common health issues. Like most people my age I suffer from common ailments. I have high cholesterol, migraine headaches, a lot of anxiety and am depressed sometimes. I do take medicine for the cholesterol problem. I admittedly don't eat right. I enjoy steak, lamb chops, pizza, ice cream and Coca-Cola. I happen to be in good company. Warren Buffet reportedly drinks 12-15 cans of Coke daily. He, like me, doesn't drink coffee. I'm not much of a cook but I do enjoying baking cupcakes especially with my daughter. It's one of those mother daughter rituals we do, like going swimming together. I should exercise more but I don't really enjoy it so I'm in the gym only two hours a week. When I worked out with my personal trainer Angel Chion, it was easier. Then he left the area for a better opportunity which I understood. One of my big fears is falling and getting hurt. I do balancing exercises to help prevent this. However, a couple of months ago I did fall down on a sidewalk and hit my head with a lot of impact. I was bleeding from my knees, hands and forehead where I needed to have stitches. Fortunately, I did not lose consciousness. I remember every scary second of the fall.

One of my goals in life is to learn something new every day. I suppose everyone has gaps in their basis of knowledge. I recently learned about the TED Conferences. Now I've added attending one of them on my "to do in the future" list. Another smaller goal is to do at least one mundane chore each day.

The lottery win has also afforded me the time to pursue many interests. For example, I recently attended a Holocaust symposium at the University of Miami. Additionally, I've joined book clubs, attended book symposiums run by my friend Gail Rice and joined an investment club. I'm also interested in nostalgia principally the 60s and 70s and the Beatles. On rare occasions, I have time to be idle which I consider a luxury.

One of the things I like and dislike about myself is that I am organized and pay attention to details. I'm also a list maker. In fact, I may be obsessed with lists, so much so, that I actually have created a list of my lists. My brain runs wild with lists. I am trapped by my own routine of lists and chores. I am busy all the time. Yet much of it, I must admit, is unproductive.

I have so many lists it drives me crazy. For example, I write down what I wear each day so as not to wear the same clothes too often, especially if I see someone frequently (like they would notice). I make lists of what I've bought on eBay, how many times a year I get sick, new restaurants I try and other insignificant things. While some people organize coupons, I catalog the hundreds of greeting cards I've pre-bought, usually with someone in mind, for birthdays and anniversaries.

In fact, that is one of my fortes in life - sending very specific greeting cards to my friends and family. I create lists of topics to talk about when meeting with friends. Different people call for different topics. Perhaps one of my more significant lists is a list of funny things that happen when I'm with Sarah. After each visit, I email her the expanded list which we both enjoy. It points out that you have to appreciate the little moments of your life. I record all of our daily spending transactions into Microsoft Money, which is time consuming and I realize there is no need for this. The lists just fly into my head. I've kept a log of the most interesting cases of my career. Many have been published in pediatric journals and I've included some in Chapter Four and others are in Appendix "A." I keep handwritten letters from significant people in my life and now their email correspondence.

All this recording takes time, and while my old lists helped jog my memory as I've written this book, the amount of data sometimes seems overwhelming.

I also suffer from a commonplace malady called "information overload" which goes hand in hand with my list problem. Years ago the search for information meant finding reference books, newspapers, encyclopedias, going to the library, using card catalogs and viewing microfiche. Now it starts and ends with the Internet. I hope books don't become obsolete. I sit for hours at a time attempting to absorb it all. Paradoxically, it seems that there is even more print material out there. I went to my doctor's and counted many unknown to me magazine titles. There's just too much on the market. I started reading a new magazine but convinced myself not to subscribe to it. I can't read all the magazines and journals already coming to the house, let alone a new one.

I know information overload is a worldwide epidemic. Even the local and national news programs are constantly directing people to go to their websites for links, for expanded coverage and more live video. Advertisements are including QR codes for those who seek even more information. Now, I don't have time for my normal stuff! I feel it takes almost as many hours to document in detail the details of each day as it does to live it. I spend up to four hours a day trying to keep up.

Did Socrates have it wrong when he said the unexamined life is not worth living? Could it be that the over examined life like mine is the problem?

Along with the everyday lists, I've created others I hope readers will enjoy. I've mercifully limited myself to six and one continuation in Appendix "C." Some of my other lists can be found on my website http://www.shirleypress.com and in my Pinterest account.

List I: Twelve of My Favorite Old TV Shows & Characters

Some of these are leftovers from childhood. Others resonate from adulthood.

Candid Camera - where a whole generation grew up thinking that the word "candid" meant "hidden."

Leave it to Beaver - Eddie Haskell, Wally's best friend, the insincerely polite, smart alec was unforgettable. Remember remarks like, "That's a lovely dress you're wearing, Mrs. Cleaver."

Dr. Kildare - the original version of Dr. McDreamy

The Ed Sullivan Show - the closest I ever got to the Beatles was to see them on that show until I broke into Paul McCartney's house

The Fugitive - the older version of The Mentalist

The Many Loves of Dobie Gillis - Beatnik character Maynard G. Krebs

The Patty Duke Show - loved the theme song

Queen for a Day - schadenfreude at its best

Saturday Night Live - Roseanne Roseannadanna "It's always something" and "never mind". Who couldn't relate?

Friends - newer version of Happy Days

Seinfeld - Jerry's sidekicks reminded me of the characters from the *The Mary Tyler Moore Show* with Elaine as Rhoda, Kramer as Ted and George as Murray. Everything is a retread.

ER - of course, my life's career

List II: Twelve Major Historical Events during my Lifetime

Everybody who was over the age of 6 when President Kennedy was shot to death on November 22, 1963 probably remembers exactly where they were when they heard the news. I was in the 7th grade, coming up the steps from gym class. It came over the PA system. With the Challenger disaster, I was at a conference on pediatrics in Hollywood, Fla. We were watching the launch on TV. At first we didn't realize something was wrong.

JFK's assassination

The Beatles arrival in America (eleven weeks after the assassination)

Civil Rights and Martin Luther King's assassination

Vietnam

First man on the moon

Challenger explosion

Berlin Wall falls

End of apartheid

The death of Princess Di

Columbine

9/11

War in Iraq

List III: Twelve Words and Sayings That Aren't Used Much Today

I tried to find out the origin of lickety split. A few theories but nothing definitive. I predict that no one will miss this phrase.

A chip off the old block

Blacklisted

Green with envy

He's a little wet behind the ears.

Jalopy

Lickety split

Lame duck

Let bygones be bygones

Mod

Okee dokee

Scaredy cat

Small fry

List IV: Top Twelve New York City Adventures

I can't believe I'm giving away all my best secrets.

Campbell Apartment - to have a drink – tucked away in a corner of
Grand Central Terminal, it's a trip back in time.

Cathedral Church of St. John the Divine – A Byzantine masterpiece on
Amsterdam Avenue

Chamber Magic at the Waldorf Astoria Towers – a cool show

Crumbs Bakeshop for cupcakes – Mmmmm

Federal Reserve Bank (you need reservations to tour) – See where
countries from around the world stash their gold – it's billions
in bullion

Joyce Gold's tour of Harlem – A professor and author, Gold shows you
the highlights of history

Macy's – The original store at 14th Street and 6th Avenue is long gone,
but the 34th Street store, where Macy's moved in 1902 is going
strong.

New York Historical Society – for those who love Tiffany lamps

New York Public Library – a library and museum in one. I love visiting
libraries around the US.

Plaza Hotel Food Hall – an upscale version of your local mall's food
court

Teddy Roosevelt's house – the president's birthplace is a perfectly
restored Victorian home

The Forbes Galleries – High priced tchotchkes of the elite. Museum of
cool stuff like centuries old toy soldiers, vintage games, art and
illustrations.

List V: Top Twelve New Inventions during my Lifetime

I consider myself a prototype baby boomer. My generation has witnessed a hell of a lot of technical advances like the mass availability of TV. Not all new technologies are as efficient as promoted. We have electronic medical records (EMR) at the hospital. It now takes me three times longer to finish a chart with the computer than it took by hand. Okay, the documentation is more complete, but give me a pen any day of the week. It's remarkable how insidiously these devices make themselves at home in our lives. Remember when AOL charged by the minute? Doctors were some of the first to carry cell phones. It was known as "The Brick." It was heavy and expensive. Only in an emergency would you ask someone to use their phone. Now they practically throw them at you.

CDs

Cell phones

Digital cameras Where do you put the film?

DVDs

Fax machines

iPods

Organ transplants

PDAs

Personal computers and the Internet

Microwave ovens

Color TV

Video games

Walkman

List VI: Nostalgia – Obsolete, Nearly Obsolete and Bygones

This list has ballooned to more than 140 items. Here are the first 20. Some are true classics, like the candy cigarettes my dad once sold. I bet tobacco company executives long for their return. The rest of the list is continued in Appendix "C".

Air mail stamps

Air raid drills and the Cold War

Analog TV

Answering machines

Army navy stores

Atari

Automat

Banking hours 9:00-3:00 p.m. Monday-Friday

Beepers

Betamax

Black Jack and Clove chewing gum

Brand X

Bonomo's Turkish Taffy

Brownie camera

Butcher shops

Cameras using film

Candy cigarettes

Card catalogs

Car fins

Car hops

Lists are more than just a series of items. They can reveal patterns –
like how much the world has changed or wasted time. Here's an example:
I kept track of how much time it took me to go to the physical therapist
after my shoulder surgery. I was going three times a week. It was far, so I
decided to switch to one closer to home. The new place was 12 minutes
closer; so that's 24 minutes saved plus there's no waiting, another 10
minutes saved. So I was saving 34 minutes three times a week which
added up to 102 minutes per week. So where was the time? Once it hit
me that I have over one and a half extra hours per week, I tried to put it
to better use, although I figured I probably wasted the time in the casino
anyhow.

But lists have a downside. They lead to chores. This is a fact. If you
don't make a list, then you don't know what is waiting to be done. And
once you do make the list, more chores clamor to climb aboard.

Oh don't get me wrong. I don't know if I would ever have made it
through the first years of motherhood or medical practice without lists. In
fact, this is the first time since 1973 where I've been caught up on my
projects and lists and actually have free time. I could, if I wanted to, stop
making lists. Furthermore, it was the first time in my life that I felt like I
didn't have to work.

I should be happy about this, yet I feel unjustifiably anxious. People
have been commenting for years on what I should do to fill up my day.
Thank you very much, my days remain quite full. First, I've been
catching up for years. I finally had time to catalog my stamp and coin
collections. I am disappointed in the accrued value of the stamps. It is a
fun hobby but not a good financial investment. In addition, I was able to

digitize and edit my photography and video collections.

There is a hierarchy to my chores. There are the normal, pedestrian chores of food shopping, cooking and errand running. There are the foot-dragging chores; the duty bound chores. There are the simple chores, the endless laborious (Sisyphean), the complex, and then there's the über-chore.

Yet, occasionally, I will have a whole, unplanned day and of course I usually waste it. But how nice is it to know that you can waste a day without consequence. Occasionally, a chore can turn into an adventure. For example I might run into an old friend. But generally, they pile up like a teenager's laundry and can wreck even the fun times. This is what I wrote in June, 2009:

We're leaving in two days for our summer vacation. I was so worn out by our trip to Europe two summers ago I wanted to go someplace easy. It took 26 hours to fly back from Venice and the luggage took an additional 48 hours to arrive. This vacation seems like it will be easier. Off to New York, then down to Cherry Hill, N.J. by bus to visit my mother, sister, aunt and cousins, then back to Manhattan, then off to Tanglewood in Massachusetts, then to Connecticut to visit Bill's friends and my friend Marsha, then back to Manhattan, and then back to Florida. Writing all this down makes me want to rethink the easy part.

My chore list balloons when people don't listen to me. It's not that I think I'm some kind of sage, but as the main family "chore-meister", I've learned over the years how to avoid making the kind of mistakes that give rise to more chores. Top on the list: always notice the taxi driver's name and his company so if you leave your laptop or jacket in his cab, you will have a wisp of a chance of retrieving it. We learned this one the hard way.

A few years ago, Bill and I came home from a trip.

"Do you have my laptop?" Bill asked when we got home.

"No, I don't have your laptop. I thought you had it," I replied.

Bill had left his laptop in a taxi on the way home from the airport. We didn't notice the name of the taxi company. So in the following days we called a lot of different cab companies but to no avail. Besides installing the old data into a new computer, I had to change all of my account numbers and passwords.

Then he left his man-bag at a restaurant. I had told him dozens of times not to carry so many credit cards yet he insisted on doing so. There must have been 20 different cards in the lost bag. I had asked him to make copies of his driver's license – no way did he do this. And people should always carry their keys separate from their bags. Did he do this? Of course, not. So we had to replace his driver's license, insurance cards, credit cards, two car key gadgets costing approximately $700, (why did he have to carry the two car keys with him?) his eyeglasses and our house keys. We had to change the locks. The result is mucho chores and aggravation and a $2,000 loss including $200 in cash.

Sometimes I consider charging my family members a fine for every extra chore attributable to them not listening to my advice.

Gershon has acquired Bill's ability to misplace things. He also lost his wallet. I had told him numerous times to give me back his Social Security card. Did he? Of course not, and we had to replace it at a Social Security office. It took over three hours. At least with Gershon it was just his driver's license and his Social Security card. Chores, chores and more chores.

What's the answer? I thought that it might be: don't have a family. But my single friends have the same problems. Don't work and win the lottery? That is everyone's answer anyway. Believe me, that is not the answer to the never-ending chore problem. I have no answer.

And I think about the big list, the really important list, the existential list: spend more time with those I love, make up for lost time, reverse the clock, pursue passions of youth, become an artist, finish this book and the next one I'm already planning.

And if the lists are just driving me absolutely crazy, I have decided to become more like Scarlett O'Hara and declare, "Tomorrow's another day." And another list.

13. Paperback Writer: Thoughts/Ideas, Pet Peeves, Advice and Facts

My dermatologist friend, Dr. Alam Berke, told me that after reaching 55, men continue to age chronologically and women then age exponentially. Too bad. It's scary to think of a year's worth of crow's feet cubed. Actually, another dermatologist, one of my medical school professors, gave me one of the best pieces of advice on aging. One day during rounds when I was a fourth year medical student, he pointed me out when speaking about skin types and pronounced, "Now Shirley here is going to age poorly."

This, of course, was intended to prompt one of the other medical students to ask why (as I, myself, was wondering). He went on to say that people with light skin complexions wrinkle the most.

This naturally caused me to inquire, "How can it be prevented?"

He told the group that I had to wear sunscreen every day of my life, rain or shine, to stave off premature aging. He actually scared me into doing this and I don't even remember his name. He's probably dead by now. Years later, my mentor, Dr. Larry Schachner, who also said that my skin was doomed without intervention, echoed this sunscreen advice. I took their suggestions. I never leave the house without sunblock on under my makeup, and today, people say my complexion is one of my best features.

That taught me a lesson: don't turn away from well meant advice. You have to listen, listen, listen, which reminds me of what Larry King has said, "I never learned anything while I was talking."

Accordingly, this is a chapter on thoughts, ideas, and yes, advice. This is the result of thinking about things, painful experiences and serendipitous events. It was only after winning the lottery that I had time to put it all together.

Thoughts and Ideas
Modern Life/Culture

Many of my ideas are about modern life. Ideas have a way of popping up when I'm exercising, driving or out shopping. For example, have you ever been outraged about the price of printer ink? Of course, you probably have. My printer cost $99. Black and color cartridges together cost me $47. So after two rounds of paying for ink, I've spent more on the damn ink than on the printer itself. Sound familiar? I call it the Barbie Doll Principle. For a little over $10, you can buy a basic Barbie. However, if you add in an assortment of her clothes and accessories, you've chalked up much more than the price of that original little money sucker of a doll. Manufacturers and marketers have applied this same premise to cell phones with their service contracts, accessories and apps.

Another one of my brainstorms is what I call the Häagen Dazs Syndrome, which also fills advertisers with glee. My premise is that poor people will splurge on something expensive because better off people do it too. Why not experience the best? "We're worth it!" commercials expound. Why not spend $4 to have the best ice cream around? My husband also noticed that working class patients in his practice overindulged for designer frames. It might be the first thing people notice - so why not have a great pair?

If you know me, you probably have heard me say repeatedly, "Be sensible" in addition to "Life is a series of chores". I have also coined other phrases, such as "vintage arm candy" to describe good-looking older women like Cher, and "baby bloomers" for us baby boomers sprouting, phoenix-like, as we age. Moreover, they've been joined by my terms, "baby gloomers" for individuals of my generation who are down in the dumps and "baby doomers" for those that don't intend to climb out, and have become terminally pessimistic, possibly from listening to the litany of Social Security funding, climate change and recession woes on the nightly news.

I used two of these terms in a Letter to the Editor published in the *Miami Herald* on June 17, 2005. This was after the University of Miami fired Ferne Labati then age 60, who was the head coach of the women's basketball team there for 17 years. She felt it was due to age and sex discrimination. I wrote. "I applaud Ferne Labati's fight against age discrimination. (The Labati lesson: Job Security is vanishing June 14, Sports) This is just the tip of the iceberg. Baby boomers will be turning 60 this year. This is a generation that fought for civil rights and women's rights, and against the Vietnam War. Age discrimination is the next important battle. As the baby boomers become 'baby bloomers' or 'baby doomers' we again are going to be a force."

I've also had a few inspired observations about our ever changing culture. Here is something that is more of a conclusion than an idea.

Having an unusual first name increases your chances of becoming famous. Examples: Barack, Cher, Elton, Eminem, Madonna, Magic, Oprah, and Shakira, to name a few. Some are original names from birth; others were created. You know immediately who they are. Check out my website for the complete list now tallying over 370 names. So let's say for the sake of discussion that 400 famous people have unusual first names. If there are 6,000 famous folks around, then 1 in 15, or 6.7 percent, has an atypical name. I think that is a high batting average.

Missed Ideas

During my life, I've come up with many thoughts and ideas. Some good, some bad and some ahead of their time. No, I didn't think of Starbucks, bottled water, bagged lettuce, Post-its, exercise clothing or some other major creation we can't live without. However, thinking that placing expiration dates on products was a good plan was one of my ideas. I remember going into my in-laws' basement many years ago and noticing canned goods that must have been decades old. Some people who lived through the Depression tend to hoard food. However, unless a can was bulging, there was no way to tell if the food had spoiled – besides getting sick from it. I thought expiration dates were needed. Of course, I never initiated this brainchild and credit for this goes elsewhere. Now they are a fact of life.

Another inspiration, which came after the lottery, was to write about charities. As I said before, the subject is truly confusing and my concept was to write a book to clear up issues about where to give, how money is used and other donor concerns. However, Bill Clinton beat me to the punch in his book *Giving: How Each of Us Can Change the World.* Charity Navigator, one of the websites that tracks non-profits on a number of indicators, did so as well.

Yet sometimes there are events or opportunities that you can't foresee. Take the Beatles cards my father sold in his grocery store in 1964 and 1965. Who knew they would become collector items? I am a self-proclaimed Beatles maven. Probably not as fervent as some, but very enthusiastic – who else do you know who has actually been *inside* one of their homes? I have read five books about the Beatles. And I also have a complete collection of the original Beatles cards. In fact, the packs of cards that my father sold for a nickel are now fetching up to $100 each if the gum is still inside. With 24 packs to a box, the packs with the box would be worth approximately $2500. Yet I didn't have the foresight to keep even one box. Again who knew? I own one intact pack that I bought on eBay just for nostalgia.

Bad Ideas

Sometimes I ruminate over bad ideas of the past such as the candy cigarettes, mercury thermometers, switching left-handed people to right-handedness and of course the new Coke. Other times I feel that a solution has been discovered and then the problem to be solved is then created. An example of this would be Febreze. This product is intended to rid odors from clothes and furniture. How about soap, water and perfume?

Also, some of my ideas just didn't work out. Take the movie club I started. The premise was simple. On the first Monday evening of each month, a group of baby boomer women recruited by me would go to the movies and afterwards dine in an adjacent restaurant. Couldn't be easier or more convenient. Everybody lived close by. Every time I organized an outing, I would get approximately 10 to 12 affirmative RSVPs. Yet on the day of the movies, the excuses, some very creative, filed in and usually only three or four would show. My friends Lori Mishcon and Jan Cantor were stalwarts, attending most of the time. After a year, it was time to let it bite the dust when, a couple times, only two of us showed up. My movie club was the New Coke. Naturally, after I dissolved it, people would come up to me and say, "What happened to the movie club? I loved it." Well, you didn't love it enough to show up!

Making up for Lost Time

Post-lottery thinking brought another realization. On some occasions, you can make up for lost time, in ways both big and small. I had wanted Frye leather boots since I was 18 years old and envied the rich girls in college who wore them. They were almost knee-high, with rounded toes, two inch wooden heels and an intricate cut out pattern stenciled in the leather. They were part cowgirl, part hippie, nothing like today's stiletto models. I could never afford them, don't even remember what they cost back then and had long forgotten about them. Fast forward to January, 2004. Bill and I had rented a car, dropped Sarah off at Cornell and then drove to New York City.

On a blisteringly cold day, Marsha, my oldest friend, and I met in Manhattan and we ventured to SoHo, an artsy part of town, to wander the shops and galleries. Suddenly they appeared – the Frye boots that had eluded me since college. Thirty-five years later my taste hadn't changed. We went into the shoe store and I told Marsha about my old longing for the Fryes.

"Just buy them. Remember you can afford them now," she said.

As I whipped out my credit card, I wondered if I would enjoy them or was it too late? Well, the answer is YES, YES, YES. I love wearing them. I even bought a second pair in teal. Better late than never is definitely true.

Here's another example. I didn't have a camera when I went to the New York World's Fair in 1964 and 1965. I've always regretted that. I was mesmerized by the fair's portrayal of what was out there in the wider world. I never forgot those experiences. In 2008, I ventured back to the grounds of the fair and Bill took pictures of me at the Unisphere, the gigantic steel globe that still stands. I uploaded this photo to my Facebook profile. Maybe you can't go home again, but you can go to the fair (or at least to the fairgrounds) again.

Of course, working part-time and having a healthy bank account eases the way to making up for lost time. I'm grateful that I can frequently visit my daughter in New York even though we talk a lot on the phone. During my visits, we spend lots of time walking the city and doing mother daughter stuff. I particularly recall a day spent exploring Central Park. We went to the Belvedere Castle, the observatory, the zoo, the mall and Strawberry Fields. It seemed as though she was a little girl and I was a young mother. Furthermore, I felt as if I was making up for some of those days when I was working so hard when she was little. We videotaped our journey and had a blast. Just another example of how my life has changed.

Less profound, but filling in the blanks all the same: watching TV shows I missed the first time around, when I worked 50 hour weeks and came home to a "second shift" of making dinner, spending time with the kids and helping them with homework. So after the lottery I began watching reruns of *Seinfeld*, *Friends*, *Everybody Loves Raymond*, and *Will & Grace*. If I watched all four, that was two hours of my day. However, it was usually late night when I was tired. So while I don't know whether those hours can reasonably be counted as potentially productive, I can file them under *"Making Up for Lost Time: The TV Edition"*.

I've also had time to cultivate new friendships. I worked with fellow physicians Abby Pudpud and Richard Couce for years but we never met socially. For the past three years, we've made an effort to get together monthly for lunch and it's great. We try to sample the newest restaurants that are always springing up in South Florida. Again, better late than never.

Several years ago, I visited a younger colleague, Shaindy Aber, who was preparing to return to her pediatric practice after having her third baby. She would also soon begin a dermatology residency. She told me her worries about how she would be able to do it all. I knew someone that determined would be able to manage. Her children might be shortchanged here or there, but I reassured her that she will do it all and then if necessary, *can* make up for lost time.

Some chances, of course, slip away for good. You can't go back and really pay attention in French class, then spend your 20s living in Paris. The same deal goes for playing musical instruments well and being proficient in sports. You have to start early. Moreover, that brings me to another one of my mottos, "if an opportunity is knocking, let it in."

Thoughts in General

Although I think I my thoughts are unique, I sometimes find my insights coming out of the mouths of others. With 78 million baby boomers out there, that's bound to happen, though I sometimes wonder if it's a kind of psychic phenomenon. *The New York Times* seems to channel many of my thoughts. Some examples: an article on how librarians have changed from the little old lady with a pencil in her hair to hip techies, usually male; a story about Krakow, Poland being a city with everything Jewish, except genuine Jews, which is exactly what I thought when I visited; a piece on how air travel delays are much worse than the carriers report, which reinforced my suspicions; and the paper also ran a story about how mother daughter ties are strengthened by the cell phone, a thought that had already occurred to me many times over.

Nora Ephron, in particular, seemed to echo my musings. For years, I have been saying that email, which evolved in the early 1990s as a convenient way to replace the personal letter, has become a huge nuisance. On July 1, 2009, *The New York Times* published her essay on *The Six Stages of E-mail*, which basically said the same thing. It may have been Nora at the pen, however, our brains were thinking in sync. Too bad she died early.

I recently wrote a one page bio of my friend, Stephanie, for her 50th high school reunion. She had four pages of "stuff" to condense for the event's commemorative book. I did a bang-up job for her - terse, witty, funny and a reflection of who she really is. I applauded myself and got rave reviews from others. At about the same time, I saw Adam Sandler's movie, *Don't Mess with the Zohan*, about an Israeli intelligence agent who moves to New York to become a hairdresser. The movie started off fine but faded after 45 minutes and never recovered. What's my point? It's relatively easy to write short and sweet. But a whole book – or a whole movie -- now that's a different story.

I have had letters published. One, in particular, was published in *The NY Times*. I commented on a story about the trend of career women stepping off the corporate track in order to care for elderly parents. According to the article, many women find it as an opportunity to leave competitive and stressful working environments. I wrote:

To the Editor:

For many career women, caring for elderly parents may be a second chance at "having it all." Feeling that they might have missed the caretaker part of life, they now have the opportunity to experience this while in turn helping their parents. Having a career and a family does not have to be traditional or in some kind of predetermined order.

Shirley Press
Hollywood, Fla., Nov. 24, 2005

Numbers

I think about numbers a lot. For instance, what is a trillion dollars? We throw around terms that few understand. If I got it right, a trillion dollars is $1,000,000,000,000. That's a million million. So, if you divide a trillion dollars by all of us 304,000,000 people living in the United States, that's $3289 per person. If I were in charge of the economy, my first step would be to give a trillion dollars to the people and see what happens to the economy. My hunch is that the people who are frugal would continue to be frugal and the spendthrifts would blow their funds in no time.

Ideas in Medicine

In the mid 1980s, I knew there was a need for a textbook on the emerging field of pediatric emergency medicine. With a full-time job, two kids and a husband, there was no opportunity for me to write a book, let alone find time to brush my hair. So the inspiration for the textbook got lost somewhere between Little League and homework. How does Angelina Jolie do it?

I was, however, successful at writing medical papers. In 1994, I had two research papers published that proved the obvious: emergency rooms staffed 24 hours a day with attending physicians – doctors who had finished their training and were licensed – would reduce both malpractice claims and payouts. The tradition had been to allow residents, helped by interns and medical students, to oversee most hospital activity on nights and weekends. Attending physicians could be reached at home if the resident thought it was necessary. Giving doctors in training responsibility was considered the best way to turn them into competent practitioners.

The decision to staff Jackson's ER with attending physicians around the clock was, in part, the result of the 1984 death of Libby Zion, the daughter of well-known New York journalist Sidney Zion. He charged that his daughter's death was directly attributed to a lack of supervision from senior physicians.

Hospitals were already moving toward increasing attending coverage, but the Libby Zion case was a catalyst. As the Pedi-ER director, I sat on a committee that came up with a plan to implement coverage changes for both the pediatric and adult ERs. Jackson increased its part-time attending coverage to full-time in 1987. But it was an expensive proposition for the hospital. Licensed doctors earn about four times what interns and residents are paid.

I thought, "How do you objectively prove that patient care will be better?"

One way, I theorized, was to see whether increased staffing correlated with a decrease in filed lawsuits and malpractice payments.

My research showed an 18.5 percent decrease in malpractice claims filed, plus a 70.1 percent reduction in award payments stemming from cases in the adult section of Jackson Memorial Hospital's Emergency Department in the two years (1987-1989) following full-time coverage.

I also determined that the malpractice payouts were reduced by 44.3 percent from cases that originated in the Pedi-ER in the three years (1987-1990) after we introduced full-time coverage. The papers were published in the peer reviewed *Journal of Emergency Medicine* and *The Archives of Pediatric and Adolescent Medicine*. Many "throw away" (this means free) medical newspapers picked up on the articles as well. Patient care was improved and the decrease in malpractice suits filed was a major way to confirm this. These articles are one of the highlights of my career.

I was also ahead of the curve in reporting the relationship between child abuse and the use of crack cocaine. In 1988, *The Journal of the American Medical Association* published one of my letters to the editor titled *Crack and Fatal Child Abuse*. It was an early alert to the devastating correlation between crack use and severe child abuse. My last line was, "The problem of crack addiction must be one of our top priorities." That was long before I would discover the ravages of cocaine abuse up close and personal, through my son.

Pet Peeves

Now for my pet peeves. I hate it when a movie leaves you hanging. Take, for example the movie *Doubt*. You watch the entire film and you still have "doubt" about the outcome. Though I guess, they did give you a clue with the title. Another annoyance is people who don't call back. With call waiting and cell phones, people can't lie about trying to call you back anymore.

I don't know whether it's the wisdom of maturity, or having the time to think, but there are a few trends that *really* annoy me. Take the saying, "Sixty is the new forty." You can't imagine how many times I've heard, this. Sixty is not the new forty. Sixty is actually the new sixty. Well, you may fool yourselves, but you can't fool Mother Nature. Practically all my friends within my age group need reading glasses, complain about wrinkles, color their gray hair and are on a statin (to lower cholesterol) medication. Besides which, arthritis is hitting our generation like gangbusters and ironically the ex-athletes seem to be hit the hardest. As an aside, my husband, a retired optometrist, prescribed one weak contact lens for one of my eyes and a stronger one for the other. Therefore, I've been spared one common baby boomer affliction: bifocals.

If you know me well, you know not to get me started on all my pet peeves. I acknowledge that I have episodes of chronic whining better known as being a consummate "kvetcher". I love to rag about May-December unions, husbands, aging being particularly hard for women and the women's movement not addressing the social concerns of women. That may seem like heresy to many but let me explain.

What about the women's movement? It did a hell of a lot for women in the fields of education, the workforce, possibilities in life and politics. However, it failed in the social arena. Author Susan Faludi has said that the women's movement was not about happiness. She is right. Research suggests that women today are more empowered, but less happy. It's hard to say why. Continued sexism? Too high expectations? Doing the lion's share of housework and childcare, even with full-time careers? Also the mindset of America has to change. Women, let's say for argument, 50 and older, are just not deemed desirable. Older means invisible in the dating world. This again has a lot to do with the fact that men die younger and no movement can fight that. Men can get younger women and so they do. If the situation was reversed, there would be many unattached men competing for women and they would even consider women older than themselves, which few men do today. In the popular book *Water for Elephants,* the protagonist is a 93 year old residing in a nursing home. He observes what a rarity he is. He wily stated that he is surrounded by what he describes as "a sea of widows."

Meanwhile, I have other pet peeves that can be more easily remedied. My utmost exasperation is when someone does not say "thank you." Okay, I can overlook the 16 year old cashier at Big Lots (and yes, I do go to Big Lots and Walmart and still clip coupons) but when it's something major, I am left flabbergasted. Being totally unappreciated is the worst.

An old colleague of mine was sued for malpractice and faced possible suspension of his medical license. Not only did I refer him to the right malpractice lawyer, I testified on his behalf. The case was settled and he retained his license. My involvement was career saving. Not grateful is an understatement. Not a note, not a gift, not a call, not a flower. Nothing. The only thing I can think of is that he was too embarrassed. I am not alone in this. According to an article in *New York* magazine, May 14, 2012, Professor Cornel West made many appearances stumping for Senator Obama in 2008. Incredibly, West received neither a thank you phone call nor a ticket to the inauguration. Plus, how about the woman who donated a kidney so that her boss could get a transplant and then got fired. What a world!

Enough about my pet peeves and things that irk me and on to advice.

Advice

I must admit I do give good advice. First and foremost: live below your means if possible. I have always done this even way before the lottery. That way you always have something extra.

I give medical advice all the time. It is one of the consequences of my calling in life. In fact, I once tracked the number of times I gave medical advice to friends or family – or even mere acquaintances – for a period of two weeks. It totaled 15 times. That's about once a day. It doesn't matter what field of medicine the problem entails, though I always give a caveat that if it's not about pediatrics, I'm not an expert. People don't seem to mind. I have helped people with bleeding (from all imaginable areas) headaches, backaches, abdominal pain, dizziness, etc.

I have saved people from surgery with prudent advice, informed people about organ transplants as the true expert I have become, rendered second opinions and innumerable times have gotten folks to the right specialist. I am a medical matchmaker. That goes with the territory.

I recently solved a medical mystery. A friend's daughter started to have tremors. After two neurologists saw her and all her tests and scans were negative, there was no diagnosis. I asked my friend if her daughter had recently received the Gardasil vaccine. She said that she had. I told her that there were many side effects from that vaccine and tremors were one of them. She emailed me back a few days later and told me that I had solved the case. Her daughter's tremors eventually resolved. That made me feel good. Nancy Drew again.

It's a hit or miss situation with people listening to my advice. Furthermore, sometimes my advice doesn't work out. For example, my son has artistic talent and has created lovely pieces using welding techniques. So I thought he might become an industrial welder. Gershon enrolled in technical school but could not stand his teacher. He does not do well with army sergeant types, so he dropped out. What do you know? *The New York Times* published an article June 24, 2009 on the high demand for welders despite the recession.

I have a suggestion for retailers. Three times in one week, I encountered problems with sales clerks not being able to navigate the cash register. Once it was a return, once it was issuing a gift receipt and the third time it was using a coupon along with a discounted price. Okay, the cash register isn't your father's NCR register anymore. And yes, it is a computer. But I don't like waiting. Needless to say, I could feel my blood pressure rising waiting for the clerks to finish these transactions. Hey Macy's, either sharpen up your employees or get simpler registers. That is my advice to retailers.

Now my advice to customers: You can negotiate in more stores than you'd expect. Just try it out. I don't like getting ripped off. I believe in value for your money. So, before I go shopping for a specific item, I check the Internet for possible coupons and discount offers. I was recently shopping with my daughter at Banana Republic and, knowing that competitor J. Crew offers a 15 percent discount for students, I asked the Banana Republic sales cashier if they had a similar program. The clerk misunderstood my question and replied, "Yes, we have a senior discount" and then proceeded to give it to me. That didn't do much for my ego, but hell, 10 percent off is 10 percent off! Now I usually ask if there is a senior discount in various stores.

Some people may not know about price adjustments. Many department stores and shops such as the Gap have this policy. If you buy something and the price is reduced within ten days or so, the store will refund the difference if you show your receipt. Not bad. Check out employer discounts and discount clubs such as AARP, AAA and Groupon. Last, but not least, if you think the price is too high, use the iPhone app Red Laser that scans the barcode and displays the item's sale price culled from various Internet sites. Even millionaires like bargains.

Plus do your research. During a cruise to Scandinavia we were planning to see Edvard Munch's painting *The Scream* at the Munch Museum. As it turned out, the Munch Museum was a half-day excursion. One of our dinner table mates remarked that if our interest centered on just that work, we could see one rendering of the painting for free at Norway's National Gallery in Oslo. It turns out that there are four versions with two at the Munch Museum. We decided to go to the National Gallery instead having more time to roam the city.

Sometimes I follow my own advice. Just try it – you have nothing to lose. I went to an event in which former Vice President Al Gore and his wife at the time Tipper were attending. My own agenda for that evening was getting a photograph with one of the them. Resolute of purpose, I combed the area for either of them. Toward the end of the cocktail hour, I spotted my prey. Tipper was easy. I immediately asked her to pose with me and of course, she was gracious. Done.

Al was tougher. I thought I might lose the window of opportunity if his entourage rushed him into the auditorium. Therefore, I moved in fast. After introducing myself, I declared that a photo with him would mean so much to me. Consequently, he also graciously agreed to pose. It made me think that with enough determination, you can achieve your goals. Then my inner cynical voice warned, "Don't aim very high and it's possible." Like many self-help books decree, lower your expectations and you too will succeed.

Of course, while I counsel others to heed advice, there is some I haven't followed. I usually write when I have finished all my chores for the day. Bad idea. Since it's an ongoing struggle to get everything done, writing takes a backseat and I do not write for days or weeks on end. I just have to make it a priority and simply do it. Arranging my thoughts takes work. Moreover, sometimes describing an event takes longer than actually living it. I figured if I could write one page per day then I would have completed this book in nine months. I obviously did not listen to my own advice.

Little Bits of Advice

If you remember nothing else from my story, but some of these tidbits, it will have all been worth it to me.

- Place an extra flash drive of your computer contents in your safe deposit box.

- Do not get into a Home Depot line behind someone buying lumber.

- Wear socks to airports.

- Order extra birth certificates and death certificates. You will need them more often than you think.

- Make sure your US Savings Bonds have not matured past their interest bearing days. It can be 10 to 40 years depending on the series.

- To have the Heinz 57 ketchup pour out quickly, tap the side of the glass bottle where the "57" is embossed.

- Make a list of questions and concerns when you have a doctor's appointment.

- Make your kids do chores.

- Use the perfume strips you find in magazines as sachets for your clothes drawers.

Facts

I guess I collect facts just as I used to collect coins and Beatles cards. Here are some of my favorites.

People in the US spend 54 billion dollars each year on lottery tickets. It's not a good investment unless you have a stroke of luck.

Do you remember when airplanes, restaurants and other places had smoking and no smoking areas? This ridiculous concept we accepted as normal. As you know, the smoke would just be blown your way anyhow.

TV facts: I was surprised to learn that *The Jetsons* TV show was originally a flop. It premiered on the evening of Sept. 23, 1962 against *Dennis the Menace* and *Walt Disney's Wonderful World of Color* and only 24 episodes were produced. It was canceled after one season. However, its influence is undeniable or as we would say today, it went viral. These original episodes were aired again in 1963 on Saturday mornings. Then in 1985, Hanna-Barbera created 41 new ones and the rest is history.

Fred and Wilma Flintstone, on the cartoon series *The Flintstones* (1960-1966), were the first TV couple to be seen sharing a bed.

Little Bits of Facts

- The first item sold after being scanned with a UPC barcode was in 1974 on a packet of Wrigley's gum.

- The first emoticon :-) was created by Professor Scott Fahlman in 1982.

- On Father's Day there are more collect calls made than on any other day in the year.

- Desserts is "stressed" spelled backwards.

- The star (*) next to a number or letter in an elevator means the ground floor. I've seen it as *1 (first floor), *M (main), *L (lower level), *G (ground) *S (street) and *C (casino on the first floor).

- The United States is probably one of the few countries where the rich breastfeed their babies and the poor generally do not.

- On Interstate 95, if the number placed before 95 is odd, the highway runs east and west. If the number is even, the road travels north and south. For example, I-295 runs north-south.

- It is impossible to lick your elbow.

- There is a strip on the left side of the US $20 bill that lights up under ultraviolet light.

- The song "American Pie" is a tribute to Buddy Holly.

- Etsy is a website for homemade and vintage goods. Now if I wanted a handmade potholder, I'd make it myself. If you had asked me to invest in this business, I would have given it a "no" vote hands down. Who knew it would grow to be a one billion dollar entity?

- The state with the highest percentage of people who walk to work is Alaska.

- The cost of raising a dog to the age of 12 can be $4,620 to $32,990.

- The number 2,520 can be evenly divided by numbers 1, 2, 3, 4, 5, 6, 7, 8, 9 and 10.

- If you were to spell out numbers, how high would you have to go until you would find the letter "A"? Answer: one thousand.

- $111,111,111 \times 111,111,111$ or $(111,111,111)^2 = 12,345,678,987,654,321$

- The first novel (that we know of) ever written on a typewriter is The Adventures of Tom Sawyer.

- Each king in a deck of playing cards represents a great monarch from history: spades is King David; hearts is Charles after Charlemagne; clubs represent Alexander the Great and diamonds is Julius Caesar.

- Half of all Americans live within 50 miles of their birthplace.

- When taking antibiotics, eating yogurt or taking probiotics may prevent diarrhea.

- The cheapest way to go from JFK Airport to Manhattan is by way of the Air Train which drops you off at a subway line that goes into the city. Combined cost: $7.50. It can be a bit of a schlepp so it's best for those without a lot of luggage.

- My favorite iPhone apps is the inflation calculator, which tells you what something in the past would cost today factoring in inflation and vice versa.

- Rubik's cube hit in 1974 followed by the Pet Rock in 1975.

- To make your own lemonade in a restaurant, ask for a glass of water with a slice of lemon and just add Splenda.

- Every year Beloit College publishes its mindset lists http://www.beloit.edu/mindset/ – a pop culture history list of what the current crop of freshmen have or have not experienced in their lives.

- Poetry writing has become easier with the rhyming dictionaries on the Internet, though I was writing poems way before.

The Internet is a trove of clever insights. Here are examples of those that others have sent me via email.

Insights

- In the United States we leave cars worth tens of thousands of dollars in our driveways and keep useless junk in our garages.

- Why do drugstores have their pharmacies in the back and have sick people walk the distance while having cigarettes available at the front counter?

- Why is lemon juice made with artificial flavor while dishwashing liquids are made with real lemons?

- One of my favorites. Why don't they make the whole airplane out of the indestructible material used to construct the black boxes?

- And now my absolute favorite. Why don't we ever see a headline that reads "Psychic Wins the Lottery."

Abbreviations and Acronyms

Onto abbreviations and acronyms. I myself have used them on occasion without knowing what they stand for. There are also websites devoted to acronyms.

- The topiary (flowers and hedges sculpted into figures) of the Disney characters at EPCOT (Experimental Prototype Community of Tomorrow) is fun to see.

- Many organizations have initials as their name. Take TMZ, a division of Time-Warner, the celebrity news website. The letters stand for "thirty-mile zone" which is a radius of 30 miles from the intersection of West Beverly and North La Cienega boulevards in Los Angeles. Shooting TV and movies within this zone is considered local and outside this zone warrants additional charges.

- IKEA stands for Ingvar Kamprad Elmtaryd Agunnaryd, the initials of the founder of the Swedish home furnishing giant and its original location.

- Laser means Light Amplification by Simulated Emission of Radiation.

- JPEG stands for Joint Photographic Experts Group.

- SCUBA is an acronym for Self-Contained Underwater Breathing Apparatus.

- RADAR stands for Radio Detection and Ranging.

- GI stands for Government Issue. GI is now used as a synonym for soldier.

- DVD used to stand for digital video disc and now stands for digital versatile disc.

- Some acronyms have multiple meanings like LOL: lots of luck, lots of love, laugh out loud and more.

- PA systems like the ones used in junior high stand for Public Address.

- Wi-Fi stands for wireless fidelity

- SWAT stands for Special Weapons and Tactics

- ROTC is the Reserve Officer Training Corps located on college campuses

- Blog means a Web log.

- Snark is a combination of snide and remark

- YAHOO stands for "Yet Another Hierarchical Officious Oracle."

- YOLO is an acronym for "you only live once".

And then there is the backronym. This is a reverse acronym when words are devised to fit initials. Take the example of the APGAR score for assessing newborns. This scoring system was named after Dr. Virginia Apgar. Appearance, pulse, grimace, activity, and respiration were the words assigned years after her publication of this score, making this an example of a backronym.

Finally, I couldn't leave this chapter without two of my favorite jokes.

- She was my best friend for 20 years and I was hers for the first two weeks -- Milton Berle

- You don't seem to be yourself lately and I've noticed the improvement -- Henny Youngman

14. Getting Better All the Time: What I Have Learned

People ask me all the time: Do you ever think what your life would have been like if you hadn't won the lottery? Of course I do. I think about that parallel life all the time. Here's how it would have likely played out. I would have stayed as the Pedi-ER director until Sarah finished college. At that point, I would have switched to working part-time, a plan I thought about long before the win. In the social aspect of life, I would probably have retained more friendships because there would have been nothing of which to be envious.

As an aside, the lottery experience has helped me understand the powerful emotion of envy and recognize it in others. Having experienced it myself in other aspects of my life, I am aware of how draining and stressful it can be.

Without the lottery, Bill would have kept his optometry practice until his liver failed. Then, assuming he would still have gotten a transplant in time, he would have probably worked part-time or gone on disability because of his decreased stamina. The kids would likely be doing pretty much the same as they would have planned to do without us winning the lottery.

I wouldn't have mastered the ins and outs of charity boards, attended high-end fundraisers and learned how to spot scammers. I might not have made the time to track down information and write about my parents' lives and obviously, would not have had the story that forms the core of this book. Another thing I did was to go on a medical mission to the Dominican Republic last year. I always had an excuse for not doing this. Then the right opportunity presented itself and I participated in the Medical Students in Action's trip as a pediatrician.

Of course, there's the writing of this book which would have not happened. The book has brought a lot of new experiences into my life. It has been an opportunity and a journey. Ernest Hemingway once stated, "It is good to have an end to journey toward; but it is the journey that matters, in the end." I must admit that the journey has been bumpy. The course of writing the book itself did bring me into unique situations, which wouldn't have happened otherwise. I met so many wonderful (and then some not so wonderful) people. However, the journey has brought me intense feelings of defeat. I'd go to bookstores and libraries and see all the books and wonder why my book has gotten rejected so many times. One agent told me that ten years ago she would have taken me on but the publishing world has changed. Another agent informed me that there is no interest in a lottery winner. While another one maintained that there's no money to be made with an unknown author. It is still a rude awakening especially for someone like me who is usually successful with enough effort.

On the positive side, I do have a fan club of at least two, Jill and Lori, who tell me, "Don't give up." During this journey, I encountered many people who said they wanted to, or were going to, write a book but haven't so far. I basically try to give them encouragement to "just do it" like a Nike ad.

Other benefits from writing this memoir are that I have spoken with many people from my past - several of whom have recently died so I'm glad I got to interview them in time. Writing the book is a springboard of sorts. I've reunited with my second cousins Betty Ettinger's daughters Lynne, Judy and Laurie whom I haven't seen in decades. I met Robert Kalish, his wife Susan and son Evan when I was in New York. It's an interesting crew of relatives. Recently, I met for the first time my second cousin Ziva who grew up in Israel. Even though she has lived in Florida for many years and we could have met years ago, I have to think that this was the right time for us. On one hand, I feel very happy for these reunions as an offshoot of my journey. On the other hand, I feel sad that we were all MIA for decades. I've reconnected over the phone with second cousins Peter Schwimmer and Wendy Kalish. The one thing I know is to approach the reconnections with no expectations. Whatever happens, happens.

Then I've met other writers like Cindy Roesel who offered me advice. I connected with Esther Herschman Rechtschafner online, an archivist from Israel whose website on Sveksna, Lithuania helped me do my research on my father's life. In addition, I spoke to Holocaust experts Dr. Miriam Klein Kassenoff and Dr. Michael Berenbaum at symposiums. When I visited the HIAS office in New York, Valery Bazarov, the historian there, was very helpful and in addition to giving me further information about my parents, he checked my chapter for historical accuracy. Madelyn Cohen of HIAS also proved to be a valuable resource.

I tried to believe that the lottery wouldn't change me. But of course it did and the transformation began the second I read those numbers off the ticket at my Miami Beach home. While I have tried to retain the core of myself and fought against some of the changes, I am not the same person I would have been. In part, this book is a way of explaining those changes to myself, as well as a legacy for my children, and I hope, one day, my grandchildren. I'm still the same sensible, loyal, committed person as before. However, as part of my growth, I am much less trusting. Having been conned a few times lent itself to this new development in my character. I try not to abandon people and that's why I continue to practice medicine. The same motivation that propelled me to become a pediatrician has not stopped. But knowing that I can walk away from my profession when work might become too stressful is a subconscious or maybe conscious alternative that I must remember others do not have. I can quit but I hope I will not do that. Just the knowing that I can walk away sets me apart. I try not to be arrogant and remember what life was like before I had money. I try to be generous in spirit in addition to being charitable. I'm there for people when it counts. I might be "full of myself" thinking like this but that is the change. It's martyrdom (sticking with the job) versus practicality (quitting the job) for me and I am totally conflicted. Not having many choices is in a lot of respects easier.

Above all, the most profound change is that I have more confidence. In addition to this, I learned that most of my new found experiences could have been done without winning the lottery. I just had to make the time. This was an epiphany to me.

One thing that hasn't changed: I'm a crier. I cry when kids die in the Pedi-ER. After 41 years I still cry when I talk about my father's early death. I cry about death in general. I cry when people tell me sad parts of their lives. I sometimes cry when I'm hurt or rejected; I just can't shrug this off. I have "rejection sensitivity" as a psychiatrist friend once told me. Sometimes it actually hurts to be who I am so I welcome someone like Speaker of the House, John Boehner to the national scene. He's much worse than I am when it comes to tears. If he was a woman, he'd be viewed as weak but as a man he is thought of as an oddity. We accept his propensity for crying. He gives hope to all of us other criers out there.

When I won the lottery, I naively thought that all my problems in life would be solved. So what does it do for you? Health, happiness and inner peace? Troubles with aging, friends, work and children? No, none of the above. What about serenity, passion and preventing disappointments? No, no and no. Does winning make you suddenly not a shy person? No. Does it promote confidence? Well yes, actually a bit. The lottery solves only one problem, though it's a biggie: financial security. I also learned that you have to appreciate all that's good in your life. Your life can change on a dime for the worse.

I am the first to admit that I was lucky winning the lottery. That's it in a nutshell. It's not karma, God's will or anything like that. I never anticipated being a lottery winner, but here I am. Winning the lottery put me in a special class with so few others – a lottery club of sorts.

Did I deserve to win? Emphatically, NO! No one deserves to win. It's a fluke event. Furthermore, this journey has confirmed my thinking on various subjects. Number one is that life isn't fair. Moreover, I've learned that there is no secret to all of this. Wishing that I won the lottery didn't make it happen. Buying tickets regularly didn't make it happen. Random luck of being at the right place at the right time did make it happen. Period.

Most of us can't know ahead of time if they will be in the right place at the right time. Or the wrong place at the wrong time. I often think about the luck people have. Some just have bad luck such as Dr. Randy Pausch. He was the professor at Carnegie Mellon and was diagnosed with pancreatic cancer at the age of 45 and died less than two years later. Unlike most in his situation, he gained national fame for his inspirational talk *The Last Lecture: Really Achieving Your Childhood Dreams*. For all his talent and charisma, his charmed life ended too soon. The same goes for Elizabeth Edwards, the wife of former Sen. John Edwards, who died of breast cancer.

I have some friends and relatives with bad luck or bad breaks in life. Some lost both their parents at an early age, a few of my friends are widows, others have cancer and one friend has a son with cancer. Some never got married which I don't really think is bad luck, unless the person really wanted to get hitched.

Having healthy, happy kids is in part good luck. People with "good" kids generally think it's a reflection of good parenting. I know better. You have to be lucky with kids. There is a lot of bad luck that will render you powerless.

My Aunt Ruchel (Tanti) had the bad luck of having a major stroke in 1998 and was paralyzed for thirteen years until her death. I regret not talking to my aunt more about her Holocaust experience. She had a better memory for facts than my mother. Tanti, who was also struck by a car in 1996, used to purchase lottery tickets. She came close one time to winning a jackpot by correctly picking five out of six numbers. She missed the sixth number by one digit.

One of our nieces has had juvenile diabetes for most of her life and just recently received kidney and pancreas transplants. Someone at the hospital once asked me if she had the same disease as my husband Bill.

"Different diseases and different transplants," I replied, but thinking that the two had something else in common – the same bad luck – negative life events you have no control over.

So I had a lucky break in life. I acknowledge this. In fact, I think everyone who is wealthy or famous somewhere along the way had a lucky break. Even the brilliant Bill Gates in his book *The Road Ahead* writes about being at the right place at the right time and seizing opportunities that came his way.

I hope I have seized the opportunities the lottery has given me, including the chance to reevaluate who I am. I know that the introspection I did when writing this book was a chance I might not have had except for the lottery. It helped me be more content with myself. But winning millions is not a pre-requisite for that to happen.

Winning the lottery has given me a chance to live out a fantasy, which I admit is pretty juvenile and immature. I like fooling people. For example: In Feb. 2007, I was attending a conference where I met an old pediatrician colleague, Dr. Michelle DeAntonio who was accompanied by her husband Mike Schneider. He was working at the time as a newsman at Bloomberg TV. Maybe it's his on camera experience that gives him so much confidence but he is definitely a charming fellow. He has what it takes. He's a talker. Mike talked to a small crowd of us for about 90 minutes. He's a consummate story teller, putting his optimistic spin on everything.

At one point Mike asked me, "Shirley, are you still the director of the Pedi-ER?"

"I stepped down and am now working part-time," I answered nonchalantly.

"Yes, politics will get you every time," was his response.

I was giddy inside. I could have updated him. But I didn't. I cagily kept the secret to myself. It was like playing a harmless practical joke.

Another time I went into a jewelry store with my friends Rose and Lois. We don't look particularly wealthy, whatever that means. The owner was in the store and didn't wait on us instead relegating us to an unseasoned salesperson. If he had known, he probably would have skitted over to us.

The best is payback. For example, the girls in Hebrew school who mocked me for being poor or unpopular – *hey look at me now*. Actually, I'm over it and should be. I've been in touch with some of them and we all "grew up".

Another instance is the rabbi from our former temple. Years ago Bill was in the hospital for kidney stones and I bumped into our rabbi on the hospital floor. I told him about Bill.

"Give him my best," he said.

Well, he could have taken five extra minutes to walk down the hall and visit Bill personally. That's even part of his job. But he chose not to. Years later, when they asked us for a sizable donation – no way.

Winning the lottery for me has repaired some wounds that go back to childhood. People who grew up without much will understand how even a well-paid doctor like me could always have anxiety about money. Winning the lottery has definitely made me more positive about life in finally putting to rest any kind of financial worry. If someone wins a big lottery and wants to contact me, they are welcome to. My first piece of advice would be to go slow. Don't make any hasty decisions.

I took my time in making changes, including the decision to step down as director of the Pedi-ER. It was a stressful job and I had been in the position for over 20 years. Yet, I stayed almost another year after winning the Lotto to tie up loose ends.

Similarly, go slow on investment opportunities that come your way. Research, research, research. Don't let the wants and needs of friends and family overcome your good sense.

Take opportunities when they present. I can't stress this enough. I try to go with the flow. I am more confident. I try to help people as much as I can. Three times while on an airplane I volunteered to assist passengers in distress.

The following was published in the comment section of the *New York Times* in response to the article "Is There a Doctor on the Plane?" by Tara Parker-Pope on May 23, 2011. It was one of 122 comments.

I was on a flight when an attendant asked if there was a doctor on board. I said that I was a pediatrician and she said that was just fine. The patient was a middle-aged man with chest pain. Another physician responded to the call.

I said to the other doctor, "Why don't you take this one since I'm a pediatrician?"

He responded, "You're closer to this case than me. I'm a retired pathologist."

So the two of us worked together and stabilized him during the flight. An ambulance was waiting on arrival.

Another flight. Another chest pain. This time it was an elderly woman flying by herself. I was the only physician on the flight. Again, I did my best to treat her. A ground control team asked me if I thought they should divert the plane. Her vital signs were abnormal but I thought she would make it to the landing. An ambulance also awaited her.

Another time it was a man who was vomiting uncontrollably. Another doctor responded and I was not chosen. I was thinking to myself, "This patient is right up my alley. I make my living off vomiting and they didn't pick me – oh, well."

Finally, rich, poor or in between, try as hard as you can when doing something. For example, I tried my best on the TLC show *Lottery Changed My Life*. I practiced with a coach beforehand. I hired a make-up person. I called the hospital to get the PR apparatus cranking away, which ended up as a front page story in *The Miami Herald*. There was only one shot at appearing on the TV program. If I had changed my mind, or had to cancel, there was no second chance.

When I was young, I felt that many of my problems had to do with lack of money. Yet, when I was blessed with having a lot of money, I saw that it brought its own set of problems. Do I give enough? When I turn someone down, I feel guilty as I can't say "yes" to everyone who asks. Hey, I'm not Oprah. I've reconciled this with myself. I've come to accept that I'm pretty good and that's good enough.

My life has been ordinary and extraordinary at the same time. I've had my share of good and bad luck. I've had gains and I've had losses. I was raised by parents who survived the concentration camps during World War II. I became a physician, wife and mother. I am a lottery winner, my husband had a liver transplant, my son is struggling with drug addiction and I am still struggling to find myself. I'm a work in progress. I try to look young, dress young and feel young although many days I feel my age. Yet day to day, my life is full of chores (good and bad) and routine aggravations like everyone else, I assume.

I can say this with confidence. Money is conflict. When I didn't have any, I resented those who did. When I had the right amount, I resented having to work so hard to get it. So now that I have lots of it, I know people resent me. In life, as in the lottery, you gotta play if you want to win. This is the journey and randomness of my life.

So as for a summary of what I've learned from my journey, I've compiled yet another list.

Shirley's Top Twelve Things Learned from Winning the Lottery

1. Life is unfair, although I've always known this.

2. Family and friends are more important than having a lot of money.

3. Age and health are life's great equalizers.

4. Money doesn't shield you from life's adversities.

5. The friends worth keeping are those who are there for you in good times as well as bad times.

6. Life is a series of chores no matter who you are.

7. Make and take opportunities even if you fail. This is my catchphrase or as they now say my platform.

8. Mixed emotions are okay and are a fact of life.

9. My calling in life remains to help people.

10. You can in some instances make up for lost time.

11. Many or most of the new things I've done since the lottery could have been done without the money.

12. I have learned to accept my sensible, overly sensitive, non-charismatic self. "Be sensible" is me.

Appendix A: Medical Cases

Among the many lists I've kept are a compilation of memorable cases that came through the Pedi-ER doors. Disclaimer: some of the descriptions of the cases are graphic in nature.

Case #1: Nurse as Detective

As a third year resident, I was called to see a 4 year old girl with cancer who was being treated with cisplatin, an anti-cancer medication, which was given intravenously (IV). After her infusion was completed, her heart rate increased to 120 beats per minute, which is abnormally high (80 is normal). I ordered some tests but they failed to reveal the cause of the high heart rate (tachycardia). When it reached a critical rate of 180, I admitted her to the Pediatric Intensive Care Unit for monitoring and intervention if needed. Even after I called consultants, no one could figure out what was happening to her heart. Until...I was pulled into a dark closet by one of the nurses who told me that two vials of aminophylline, an asthma medication, were missing from the nurses' station. I was stilled puzzled. She asked if I knew what cisplatin was mixed with to make it an intravenous solution. I admitted that I did not know. She stated that it was diluted with sterile water in vials. And then the light bulb went off! Aminophylline is also a clear solution like sterile water. I dashed to the girl's bedside and immediately drew an aminophylline level. Sure enough, the level indicated that she had been accidentally infused with this medicine, which was potentially fatal not only causing a rapid heart rate, but could have caused an irregular heartbeat, seizures and death as well. Luckily, she did well and was transferred out of the ICU the next day. After solving this mystery, the labeling of IV medications on the wards was improved to prevent similar incidents.

Case #2: Child Abuse

A 4 year old boy was brought into the Pedi-ER by his mother with the chief complaint that his "inners and blood were coming out of his rectum." The child was in impending shock as we treated him with intravenous fluids and called the pediatric surgical service. His mother had brought him in and said that he had jumped on a plunger in the bathroom but later changed her story. I, myself, was mentally reviewing all the diseases that could cause the bowel to protrude (eviscerate). Well, I didn't have to wait long for the answer. The surgeons reported back that this was trauma inflicted by an object pushed up the anus, a horrible case of child abuse. The boy was operated on and his bowel was repaired. The state was called and the patient, after discharge from the hospital, was released to his grandmother under the supervision of the Department of Children and Families. This was one of the worst cases of child abuse that I encountered.

Case #3: Parent's Intuition

Most pediatricians never see even one bowel evisceration in their careers. Yet I've encountered two. The other one was in a 3 week old baby brought in for a cold. The mother also mentioned that the umbilical cord looked strange to her. The other attending physician working with me on that shift decided to cut the remnant off, since it was about to fall off naturally within a few days. All of a sudden, the patient's entire bowel had eviscerated through his naval. The surgeons were again called to repair the bowel. It turned out that the patient was born with bowel tissue imbedded in the umbilical cord, a very rare condition. Had the cord fallen off anywhere but in the emergency room, this baby would have likely died. Mother knows best.

Case #4: Medical Student Topped the Docs

A medical student was examining a 9 year old patient and said to me, "Dr. Press, I think his heart is on the wrong side of his body."

I thought to myself, "If this kid really has a reversal, it surely would have been picked up before now."

The condition is called situs inversus when the body's major organs are in reversed position such as the heart being on the body's right side while the liver is on the left side. It is a mirror image of where they should be located. Situs inversus occurs in approximately one of every 8,000 people. Surely a doctor would have realized the discrepancy before the patient was 9 years old. However, I examined the boy and his heart sounds were, indeed, emanating from the right side of his chest instead of the left. I ordered x-rays and situs inversus was confirmed. Never underestimate a medical student. A "better late than never" diagnosis. I complemented him on a great find. This finding was important for the patient, his family and his doctors, so that significant medical problems in the future would not be missed.

Case #5: Déjà vu Medical Student

A 3 year old child came in with abrupt vomiting. As I was examining the patient, she kept vomiting repeatedly. I was explaining to the medical student that this could be food poisoning, an infection or an accidental overdose. The medical student then asked the mother if anyone in the household was on Tegretol, a medication used to treat seizures. She straightforwardly answered that one of her children was taking this drug -- as if it were the most routine question. I was very bewildered until the student explained that the vomitus smelled like Tegretol, which he was familiar with. How vomit could smell like anything other than vomit still baffles me but he was right. This was a case of accidental Tegretol intoxication for which we treated the patient. Leave it to these "inquiring" medical students.

Case #6: Big Surprise

A 6 year old boy arrived with the chief complaint of pus coming out of his buttock. He had been brought to another emergency room two days earlier after sitting on a pencil while in school. The wound was irrigated and he was placed on antibiotics. His parents brought him to Jackson because he wasn't getting better. I examined the wound and thought I saw the gray tip of a pencil. I ordered an x-ray, expecting to see just the tip of the pencil imbedded in the muscle of the buttock. You can't imagine my shock when on the x-ray I saw the entire pencil in his buttock tissue. It had traveled through his pants and lodged there. Even though this was rather serious, we nicknamed him "pencil boy." The surgeons extracted the pencil in the operating room and he did well.

Case #7: Another Foreign Body

I pride myself on being able to remove foreign bodies from the nose and ear canals. Over the years, I have extracted a number of items including beads, corn, coins, insects and crayons. Therefore, I presumed this was just another routine case. The patient was 2 years old and had stuck a "coin" up her nose. On inspection, it looked like the edge of a nickel. Many of the doctors including myself tried to remove this object but it would not budge. So in exasperation we called the ENT (ears, nose and throat) service to help us. They also were unable to remove it so they took the patient to the operating room. The coin turned out to be a button battery, which was retrieved before it started leaking corrosives into the nostril. That could have caused serious tissue destruction.

Case #8: Not Able to Save

A 7 year old patient was brought into the Pedi-ER in full cardiac arrest. We were unable to insert a breathing tube into her windpipe so we oxygenated her with a bag-valve-mask device. We tried our best but could not resuscitate her and she died. She had fallen off her bicycle, was found unconscious and rushed to the Pedi-ER. We thought it was a case of fatal head or abdominal trauma secondary to the fall. However, on autopsy, a piece of pizza was found lodged in her windpipe. She had apparently been eating pizza, choked while riding her bike and then fell or the other way around – fell and then choked. Either way, it was a true tragedy.

Case #9: Using my Intuition

A patient arrived at the Pedi-ER in severe respiratory distress. Many times we assume such symptoms indicate asthma and start inhalation treatments and the child improves. However, in this case the patient was getting worse. We brought the child to the resuscitation room and took x-rays of his chest and throat. The child was intermittently turning blue as we were treating him. We had trouble putting a tube down the windpipe (trachea) and the ENT resident was called. Then it hit me. There must be a foreign body in the trachea that did not appear on the x-ray. When the resident arrived, I insisted and insisted that the patient must be taken to the operating room. They finally obliged and a chicken bone was extracted from the trachea and the child was saved. Patrick Bethel, one of the technicians, accompanied the child. He returned and said, "Great job, Dr. P." It was one of my most gratifying moments.

Case #10: Déjà vu Intuition

A 15 year old teenager came to the Pedi-ER with arm swelling. He was working in shop class when a drill bit shot into his arm. His teacher pulled it out with nothing said. I have to assume it's a common experience. A few days later, his arm swelled. I examined the patient and felt a crunching sound when squeezing his arm. I took an x-ray and saw air within the muscles. I consulted hand surgery. The orthopedics fellow felt that the air was from the drill gun and it was a minor infection. I disagreed. I told him that I wanted his attending physician to see the patient. After examining the patient and reviewing the x-ray, he said three words to the fellow, "Book an OR (operating room)."

The teenager had gas gangrene, a serious bacterial infection that can destroy muscles and limbs and can lead to shock and death if untreated. I suspected this was the diagnosis though I had never come across a case before or since. Another rewarding case in my care.

Appendix B: Coincidences

Conclusions: Results May Vary

I've been interested in luck and coincidences all my life. Being at the right place at the right time has had a huge impact on me, from my Paul McCartney adventure to getting into medical school and of course, to winning the lottery. I feel that significant coincidences happen to most people. You have to recognize them and take advantage of the opportunity. I've long kept track of mine. Some refer to these as synchronicity, randomness or chance. Whatever it's referred to as, it's food for thought.

Very Unusual Events

1970: Breaking into Paul McCartney's House in London (refer to Chapter 4 - Getting Better for details)

We took photographs of the rooms, which are not available anywhere. Were we criminals? Maybe. Did we do wrong? Of course. But we were kids and zany ones at that. Who else would break into a home and admire things, not even wanting to move them an inch so that they would not be disturbed? All burglars should be that considerate.

2001: Winning the Florida Lotto

The chances of being the sole winner were estimated at 1 in 20 million. This obviously affected my life much more than the Paul McCartney house episode.

Unusual, Thought-Provoking Events

Acing my Medical School Interview in 1974

I wrote about this in Chapter 4 – *Getting Better*. This is an example of how a stranger affected my life. My intuition told me to wear feminine clothes that day and it paid off.

Predicting Death with No Experience

I was so green (Chapter 4 – *Getting Better*) when I predicted when my first cancer patient would die. I haven't been so accurate in similar situations even with a lot more experience under my belt.

Predicting Death with a Little More Experience

I told my mother in 1992 that Harry, her second husband, would probably die by choking, which did happen a few weeks later at a nursing home. A previous choking episode he had suffered clued me in.

Predicting, with Even More Experience

When my mother told me in 1994 that Rabbi Neulander's wife had been found murdered in Cherry Hill, N.J., where my mother also lived, I remarked that the rabbi probably had something to do with it.

"What you said is a 'shonda' (sin)," said my mother, outraged by the idea.

However, I was right. Years later a jury convicted him of orchestrating the whole thing and he became the first rabbi in the United States to be convicted of murder. At that point I had worked for two years with child abuse and domestic violence issues. Such work gives one a gut feeling for these things.

Wanting Someone out of your Life

This may be out of character but the following doctor tortured me for years. I'll call him Dr. Brand X. To begin with, he was the meanest son of a bitch around. He constantly criticized and berated me at work. Every time I spoke to him I would get aggravated. I would have preferred a root canal to dealing with his shenanigans. I felt like telling him off, but didn't since I feared I would lose control. He had a good position and was not likely to transfer to another hospital. However, he was obese and I always fantasized about him having a heart attack. Then he started on a diet. The pounds were shedding off at a remarkable pace. Well, actually too remarkable. He had an undiagnosed cancer which was discovered too late. In the end, I felt badly only for his family.

The New York World's Fair, 1964-1965

During the summer of 1964, when I was 13, I went to stay with my cousins the Kalishes who lived in Flushing, N.Y. The highlight of that summer was being able to walk to the fair. We went on at least four occasions and several more times the next summer as well.

The fair was a pivotal event in my life. Until then, I had never been out of New Jersey, except for a trip to Philadelphia. To go through General Motors' Futurama, General Electric's Carousel of Progress, the Kodak and the IBM exhibits and the world country sites were the ultimate experience for me. It got me thinking about the possibilities in life.

The Futurama ride was mesmerizing with its "trips" to the moon, the jungle, under the sea and to an ultramodern vision of a metropolis with a Jetsons' vibe to it. Workers at the Futurama exhibit were handing out little pins printed with the statement, "I HAVE SEEN THE FUTURE." I took some extra pins thinking that one day I would give one of the pins to someone who would appreciate it. For the next 43 years they were tucked away in a shoebox. In 2007, I found just the right person. Lawrence R. Samuel, author of *The End of the Innocence: The 1964-1965 New York World's Fair* came to South Florida on a book tour. I went to his reading and knew at once he was the person. As I was buying a copy of his book, I asked him if he had a "Futurama" pin and he said he did not. I then gave him the pin, which I had brought with me. He was surprised and very appreciative of the gesture.

Barbra Streisand Concert

In 2006, I mentioned to my friend Jill that I was going to go to the Barbra Streisand concert in Sunrise, Fla., with my friends Lori and Cheryl. She mentioned that her mother Louise was going as well.

Louise called me a few days later and said, "Shirley, I hear you're going to the concert. Where are you sitting?"

"I don't know," I replied, "My friend Cheryl has the tickets."

She gave me her seat number so that we might find each other.

When Cheryl handed me my ticket in the car, I was astounded to see that it was the seat next to Louise's. The stadium has 14,000 seats. That's a 1 in 7000 chance. Not quite the same odds as winning the lottery, but still unlikely.

Same Vacation

While out to dinner with our friends Ron and Renee, we discovered that we had signed up for the same July, 2008 Brandeis University seminar that was being held in the Berkshires. Neither Ron nor Renee went to Brandeis but had heard about this conference from other friends. We were unable to go because Bill was stricken with the liver failure that led to his transplant.

Grandmothers and Granddaughters

My mother-in-law, June, is friendly with a woman in one of the bereavement groups she joined after the death of Bill's father. June's friend boasted that Chelsea Clinton was in her granddaughter Rachel's graduate program at Columbia University. Well, that sounded familiar to June, and it turned out that Rachel, was in the same graduate class as our daughter Sarah. The grandmothers are friends and so are their granddaughters.

Relatively Speaking

A few years after winning the Lotto I joined the local chapter of the Chaîne des Rôtisseurs gourmet dining club. I was chatting with Carol Lewis who I met at one of the dinners. After glancing at my name tag, she asked if I was Jewish. Yes, I replied, and asked why she wanted to know. She told me that "Shirley Press" was her mother's maiden name.

Then she asked where my father's family was from and I replied, "Lithuania."

You could see the excitement on her face. We discovered that our relatives were both from the same country. Then the inevitable question: Are we related? She told me that she had books of family records.

The next week I went over to her house. Carol said that her family had been bakers in Europe. I responded that my father had been a baker in Dachau. Then she gave me the record books which I read cover to cover. There were some names in common, including Gershon, my father's name, and those of his brothers, Meyer, Beryl and Welrel. But there was no direct connection to my grandfather Beines Press. Undaunted, we sought out the next level – DNA testing. The testing relies on comparing Y chromosomal information, so males are the ones who must send in saliva samples. I called my father's first cousin Leon to see if he would do it and he did. For weeks we waited for the results. The DNA was not a match. I was severely disappointed. We will have to settle for being cousins in spirit.

One for the Sit-Coms

I left my orthopedist, "Joe," because the shoulder surgery he performed failed to adequately improve my pain. Instead, I went to see a shoulder specialist at Jackson, let's call him "Stan." As the new orthopedist and I were leaving the exam room, another doctor ran up to me and exclaimed, "Shirley Press!" I vaguely recognized this doc but didn't recall his name. I slyly caught a glimpse of his ID badge and realized it was Joe's brother, "Mike," who had just taken a job at Jackson. He is also an orthopedist who trained at Jackson many years ago. Now Stan, my new orthopedist, and I both know I ditched Joe, but what are the odds of the two of us together running into my former orthopedist's brother? It was like a *Seinfeld* scene. I had a weird feeling of getting "caught." I always wondered if it got back to Joe.

Jill and Bill (as in Clinton)

In 1993, I happened to enter Books & Books on Lincoln Road in Miami Beach just as a local author began reading from her newly published book, *From I Do to I'll Sue*, about celebrity divorces. The author's name was Jill Bauer. I ended up staying for the entire presentation, and then bought a copy of her very amusing book. Fast forward to June, 2004. I'm in line at Books & Books in Coral Gables, waiting for Bill Clinton to sign his autobiography. The South Florida heat was miserable, making the wait seem even longer. I came across an air-conditioned vestibule and took a break from the line while my friend Cheryl held my place.

"You look familiar," said a woman, also there to find relief.

We exchanged names, and I remembered she was the author I'd heard speak nearly a decade earlier. We talked and talked and it was the beginning of a beautiful friendship. Jill has now moved to New York and I often see her when I visit my daughter.

Triple Play

Here is a trifecta of coincidences that happened over the course of three days.

1. Cupcake Connection

I met my sister's friend Ena in Cherry Hill, N.J. Ena mentioned that a friend of hers lives in South Florida and started Misha's Cupcakes, which happens to be a favorite shop of mine.

2. Seagram's VO instead of Dough

When my mother moved to an independent living facility, my sister and I cleaned out her house. We found two unopened packages of Seagram's VO liquor. One was from 1962 and the other from 1968. Neither of us had any use for them but we thought that there must be someone out there that would really appreciate the bottles. We did not have to wait long. That evening a guy from my sister's workplace came by with his pickup truck to move some items for us. Barb gave him a thank you note with $50 inside. When he opened the card he said he couldn't take the money because he was doing her a favor as a friend. I asked him if he would like the vintage bottles of Seagram's that we had found. This could not have been a better present. He told us that he always wanted to own vintage liquor and he that had a spot waiting for them on his bar.

3. Hankie Happening

The third coincidence was when I sauntered into a shop called Muji in the Chelsea district of Manhattan. It's a unique designer store that features handkerchiefs printed with New York, London or Paris maps. I passed on the hankies and then regretted it. A day later I was at JFK Airport and there was an outlet of the store called Muji to Go. It afforded me a second chance to buy those hankies.

Lefty, Lefty and more Lefties

Both Bill and I are left-handed. The odds of being left-handed are 1 in 10. So the odds of us both being left-handed are 10 x 10, or 1 in 100. My mother was born a southpaw but it was considered bad news in Europe at the time and she was "switched" to being right-handed. One night we were out to dinner with friends Lori and Arnie and another couple. We realized all six of us were lefties. The odds of this are 10 x 10 x 10 x 10 x 10 x 10 or 10^6 or 1 in 1,000,000. This is my life.

Sarah's Turn

Birth Date Mate

Sarah was in a Duane Reade drugstore near her New York apartment. She was browsing the aisles waiting for her prescription to be ready. The pharmacist called over the loudspeaker for the customer born on my daughter's birth date to pick up her medication. When Sarah got there, she encountered another young woman with the exact same birth date. They realized this coincidence, but neither of them seized the moment to pursue a possible friendship. Furthermore, they were both holding the same exact gummy worms package, chosen from many candies in the store. I would have grasped the opportunity to befriend my birth date mate. I've never found anyone so far, born on my birth date.

The Remote Coat

Sarah and I were shopping for a winter coat. She had seen the one she liked in Bloomingdale's but wanted to show it to me before she purchased it, or shall I say before I purchased it. When we arrived at Bloomingdale's, they were completely sold out of the coat. I suggested we try Macy's. After we got to Macy's, Sarah wanted to get a hot chocolate.

"Let's buy the coat first," I urged.

We arrived at the coat department and found that there were three left in that style and her size. One was being bought by a young woman, one had a broken zipper and the last one seemingly was there for Sarah.

While Sarah was trying on the coat, another young woman came up to her and said, "Are you going to take that coat? Because if you don't want it, I'm going to take it."

We took the coat. If we would have stopped for the hot chocolate, we would have missed the coat again. Strike while the iron is hot.

Trying to Pee in Peace

Then there's the story about Chelsea Clinton and Sarah. Chelsea had enrolled in the Mailman School of Public Health at Columbia, one year after my daughter had picked the same program. I found out this little tidbit on the first day of Sarah's second year when the students were buzzing with news of the famous new student.

"This is the best thing that has ever happened to the school." Sarah exclaimed.

Everybody tried to treat Chelsea as just another student. But that didn't always work out. One day Chelsea went into the ladies room. Her body guard presumably had checked it out in advance. Then my daughter entered and said "hi" to Chelsea.

About two minutes later, Chelsea's security guard knocked on the door and asked, "Are you okay?"

Was Sarah considered a possible bathroom threat?

There you have some of the most memorable coincidences or odd happenstances of my life. My friend Renee remarked that things like this just don't happen to her. And then I reminded her of a strange event that she had told me about. Ron Gup, a pulmonologist (and our friend) left his business card on her coffee table after their first date. The following day, one of her friends was visiting and saw the card. She asked Renee how she knew Dr. Gup. She explained she had gone out with him the night before. Her friend went on to tell her that he had treated her mother for her last illness and that he was most compassionate doctor she has ever known. Consequently, Renee realized that these kinds of things do happen to her.

Life is a series of coincidences. You never know they will happen. I'm always on the lookout. "Hey Ringo, what's your address?"

Appendix C: Lists

List VI: Nostalgia – Obsolete, Nearly Obsolete and Bygones Continued

Cap guns

Car phones

Carbon paper replaced by Xerox

Cedar closets

Cell phone that's only a phone

Classified ads in newspapers

Cleats

Clotheslines

Cork pop guns

Computer punch cards

Customer service

Dictionary in print

Diving boards and slides on home pools

DOS (Disk Operating System)

Double features

Dressing up for airline flights

Drive-in theaters

Earth shoes

Eight-track tapes

Elevator men

Encyclopedias in book form like Britannica or the World Book

Esso

Five and Dime Stores

Flash bulbs

Floppy disks that were really floppy

Full-service gas stations

Fuller Brush Man

Garter belts

Hair curlers

Ham radios

Handwritten notes

Heathkits

Hitchhikers

Horn & Hardart Automat

Hula hoops

Hydrox Cookies

Ionic Breeze

Jingles on radio and TV

Juke boxes

Kodachrome film

Laundry detergent with free gifts like drinking glasses inside the box

Lead gasoline

Lincoln Logs

Lockers in airports, bus stations and train stations

Lockers at school

Long distance calls that were very expensive

Made in Japan once the emblem of shoddy products

Magazines like *Look*, *Life* and *Collier's*

Manual windows in cars

Mercury thermometers

Metal ice cubes trays with levers

Microfilm

Milkmen

Mimeograph machines

Mr. Zip for zip codes and not zip drives

Newspapers in print

Oxford saddle shoes

Paperboys

Paper dolls

Paper maps

Paper straws

Parking meters

Pay phones

Pay bathrooms

Penny candy

Pensions

Periodical Index

Pet rocks

Phone books

Phone booths

Phone numbers with seven digits and those beginning with two letters
 i.e. NO (Normandy) 7- 5555

Phone party lines

Photo negatives

Polaroid cameras and photos

Pong & Ms. Pac Man

Postage stamps that need licking

Postcards

Radar detectors

Reel-to-reel tape recorders

Roller skates with keys

Rolodex

Rotary phones

S&H Green Stamps

Saving bonds and saving stamps

Sears Catalog

Shade tree mechanics

Shorthand

Slide rule (replaced by the handheld calculator)

Slips under every dress

Small shops (appliance, bakery, camera, candy, hardware, grocery, leather goods, linen, lingerie, pet, pharmacy, record, sports, stationery and toy)

Smoking sections on airplanes, theaters and restaurants

Soap boxes (replaced by the Internet)

Soda machines that dispensed glass bottles

Spanking your child

Subway tokens

Super 8 movie camera (replaced by video cameras)

Sweetheart Soap

Switchboards

Toll takers

Toy electric irons

Trampoline parks

Turntables

TV antennas

TV commercials for cigarettes like the Marlboro Man and liquor

TV test patterns

Two dollar bills

Typewriters

Typists

Victory gardens

Video rental stores

Vinyl records

VHS

Waxed coke bottles

Walkie talkies

Washtub wringers

Watches that only tell time

Waterbeds

White gloves

Whitewall tires

Yellow Pages

Acknowledgements

There are many people to acknowledge and thank for their contribution to my book. First and foremost, I am grateful to my family who not only supported my effort, read countless versions of this memoir, edited insightfully but most importantly provided the material for the book. They are my parents Gershon Press (deceased), Leah Press Kalina, Husband Bill Rapoport, daughter and editor Sarah Rapoport, son Gershon Rapoport (who let me write very candidly about him), sister Barbara Elkan and her husband Rob Elkan, nephews Andy and Josh Elkan, niece Maddie Elkan, Aunt Ruchel and Uncle Hashel Kirschner (both deceased), Cousins Janet Coleman, Phil, Jonathan, and Jennifer Kirschner, Cousins Beverly, Jeff, Rob and Alex Simonoff, mother-in-law June Rapoport and brothers-in-law Michael and Steven Rapoport, niece Dayna Rapoport, Nephews Jonathan, Mathew, Dylan and Todd Rapoport, Cousins Marcia and Scott Weber, Sam and Marilyn Jacobs, Wendy and Robert Kalish, Aunt Margie and Bobby Solomon, and Cousins Debbie and Jimmy Keese.

My timing was good in regard to interviewing my parents' relatives and friends. I spoke to many folks just in the nick of time – Rebecca Aupperle, Leon Dworkin (deceased), Betty Ettinger, Frieda Levy (deceased), Jim Serchia, Dorothy Schwimmer, Dorothy Shatoff, Sam Sherron, and Sol Zytcer (deceased and always last when listed alphabetically).

My friend Jill Bauer provided me with unwavering support and professional advice. My thanks to Karen-Janine Cohen for her guidance through the editing and writing process. Other writer friends include Alyn Darnay, Mercedes Diaz, Diane Feen, Susan Margulies Kalish, Reina Lipkind, MD, Eva Ritvo, MD, and Cindy Roesel. Thanks to the women in my writing group: Rachel Blechman, Marian Del Vecchio, Elizabeth Fisher, Dr. Diane Goodman, Tamara Nixon and Judy Wurtman.

My friends and colleagues at work who provided me with a second "home" for more than 30 years deserve thanks. They are Hazel Adelakun, Gilbert Barguez-Aris, Joan Bender, Cynthia Bennett, Jeff Bernstein, Debbie Bess, Patrick Bethel, Marjorie Booz-Saintil, Kim Browning, Ann Campbell, John Cienki, MD, Hector Chavez, MD, Ernest Claude, Ann Coombs, Claudio Cornejo, Rich Couce, MD, Bonita Cox, Haidee DeLeon, Waltrice Fair, Nancy Fawcett, MD, Joan Franklin, Juma Gangadeen, Teresa Garcia, MD, Sondria Giordani, Maria Gonzalez, Dawn Gray, Charmaine Greene, Kim Greene, Loretta Henderson, Magalie Isma, Donna James, Merline Jean-Baptiste, Melody Land, MD, Michelle Machin, Cynthia Magnole, Michelle Martin, Shereese Martineau-Allen, Mark McBride, MD, Jacqueline Mercurius, Mirda Merisier, Claire Miguel, Kwand Mitchell, Michael Mitchell, Bettinya Petithomme, Vanessa Plunkett, Dr. Abby Pudpud, Bruce Quinn, MD,

Andrea Randley, Augusto Saintphard, Kathy Schrank, MD, Rick Sobel, Marcia Steiner, Anika Stokes, Nirit Swerdloff, MD, Akram Tamar, MD, Valerie Thompson, MD, Maria Torres, Lee Worley, MD Corafay Whylly, Dave Woolsey, MD and the rest of the Pediatric-ER staff.

My friends who deserve special thanks for hearing me talk and kvetch about this book and lending their support for years. Cheryl (Shaindy) Aber, MD, Mona Adams, Beth Albert, Linda Alexander, MD, Bev and Charlie Ashler, Ann Ballen, MD, Marilyn Baker, Rose and Larry Ben, Dina Ben-Ari, Teva Benshlomo, Drs. Elam and Bill Berke, Judy Berlin, Lori Bonnell, my book club friends, Paulette Bronstein, Jan Cantor, MD, Angel Chion, Ina Cooper, Lew Dan, MD, Ann-Lynn Denker, PhD, Margie Duarte, MD, Drs. Kay and Leo Edelsberg, Lisa and Dr. Barry Eichenbaum, Stephanie Engelberg, Mimi Folwell, Jennifer and George Fredericks, Larry Friedman, MD, Mona Friedman, Eileen Gately (deceased), Lynne Goldberg, Sofia Goldsmith, Belle and Dr. Robert Grand, Marc Grossman, MD, Ron Gup, MD, Caryn Goodman, Joni and Mel Gordon, Kim Greene, Anita Hochman, my IDF friends, Allyn and Peggy Jacobson, Danny Jonas, Fred Jonas, MD, Shulamit Katzman, MD, Susan Kelley, Jill Leslie, Cheryl Levin, Betsy Levy, Beverly Lewis, Gloria Luria, Candace Malkin, Shirley Malter, Lori and Dr. Arnie Mishcon, Dianne Parker, MD, Deena Plevinsky, Mark Polyocan, Carol and Ira Price, Patricia Rasmussen-Burgo, Lois and Larry Reese, MD, Marsha and Bernie Richfield, Gail Rice, Terry Rosen, Annette Rosenfield, Lili Rotholtz, Renee Rotta, Barbara Rutter, Arlene Sankel, Dr. Larry and Irit Schachner, Ruth Schobel, MD, Eleanor "Lenni" Seidman, Drs. Ilene and Jay Sosenko, Alissa Stein and Diane Taub.

A virtual thanks to all my Facebook friends, LinkedIn connections, Twitter guys, Pinterest followers, Instagram people, Goodreads readers and Website supporters.

I feel lucky to have all these people in my life - those who supported and encouraged me through this long haul and also promised to buy a copy of the book.

About the Author

Dr. Shirley Press is a board certified, pediatric emergency medicine physician, author and lottery winner. Dr. Press has written over 20 published articles & chapters in medical journals and books. In her memoir, *Pressing My Luck*, Dr. Press shares personal life experiences as well as the challenges and self-discoveries prompted by her Florida lottery windfall.

As the former director of the Pediatric Emergency Department at Jackson Memorial Hospital and former Associate Professor of Clinical Pediatrics at the University of Miami Miller School of Medicine, Dr. Press has 30+ years of experience treating children with acute medical conditions and evaluating victims of child abuse. Despite her lottery windfall, Dr. Press continues to work in the Pediatric Emergency Department and remains a voluntary faculty member of the Miller School of Medicine. She received her BA from Brandeis University and her medical degree from Hahnemann Medical College (now Drexel University College of Medicine) in Philadelphia. To read more about Dr. Shirley Press, go to her website http://www.shirleypress.com.

Made in the USA
Lexington, KY
09 January 2015